SOUTHWARK IN THE BLITZ

NEIL BRIGHT

AMBERLEY

This book is dedicated to the memory of Annie Lakin plus Henry and Lillian Winter.

First published 2016

Amberley Publishing
The Hill, Stroud
Gloucestershire, GL5 4EP

www.amberley-books.com

Copyright © Neil Bright, 2016

The right of Neil Bright to be identified as the Author
of this work has been asserted in accordance with the
Copyrights, Designs and Patents Act 1988.

British Library Cataloguing in Publication Data.
A catalogue record for this book is available from the British Library.

ISBN 978 1 4456 5615 1 (print)
ISBN 978 1 4456 5616 8 (ebook)

Origination by Amberley Publishing.
Printed in Great Britain.

Contents

Foreword   4

Introduction   5

The Build-up to the Blitz   8

1940: The Blitz Cometh   19

1941: A Deadly Spring   63

1942 and 1943: The Middle Years   88

1944: Small and Large Packages   97

1945: The End, but Still a Sting in the Tail   117

Appendix   127

Notes   128

Foreword

There are few areas in London with a past as long, rich and fascinating as Southwark's – and there are few areas or people as badly affected by the Luftwaffe as Southwark and its citizens during the Blitz. Attacks obliterated docks, homes, churches and warehouses stretching from Surrey Docks to Camberwell. Bombs destroyed lives, homes and communities, and the damage was long-lasting. The impact was felt for decades, and it left wastelands, rubble and disused shelters across Southwark that took decades to clear. In 2015, an unexploded bomb was found just off Grange Road, and there are likely to be more still.

But there was one thing the Nazis could not assail – Southwark's amazing people and their overwhelming fortitude. Throughout the Blitz, the people of Southwark displayed continued resilience in the face of adversity, demonstrating the spirit that ultimately kept the community together.

As Member of Parliament for Bermondsey and Old Southwark, it gives me great pleasure to represent a community that showed such tremendous courage, commitment and determination during the horrific attacks. The accounts in this book act as evidence of Southwark's own Blitz spirit, while the discussion of local research works as a fascinating narrative.

Neil Bright has established himself as one of the leading authorities of London's history during the Blitz. Accompanied by his previous publication, *A Wander Through Wartime London*, this book *Southwark in the Blitz* serves as a captivating account to be enjoyed by those seeking personal testimony and knowledge alike.

Neil Coyle, Member of Parliament for Bermondsey and Old Southwark.

Introduction

Following the release of my first book, *A Wander Through Wartime London*, with good friend Clive Harris, it had been my intention to write another. However, time and a busy schedule prevented this until recently.

I moved to the London Borough of Southwark nearly twenty years ago, having met my wife, a resident of the borough, at Southwark council. I am settled and at home here.

Ten years ago, with the guidance of Clive, a premier battlefield guide, I developed my first two guided Blitz walks, 'Bermondsey's Blitz' and 'Old Southwark in the Blitz'. These I have delivered many times to a keen and enthusiastic public. Southwark Local Studies Library was extremely helpful in assisting in the compilation of these walks and with some of the content of the book.

Modern Southwark comprises three pre-1965 boroughs as the 1899 Local Government Act was repealed in 1963. These old boroughs were Bermondsey, Camberwell and Southwark.

I wanted to look at the three boroughs chronologically through the eyes of their inhabitants and document the bravery and self-sacrifice of everyday folk. After all, from September 1940, men, women and children were now the front-line troops, who could only fight back with their cheeriness and never-say-die spirit. This book is intended to be a testament to those who lost their lives, to those who 'endured' and to those who put their lives on the line to save others.

The three old boroughs vary in their diversity and geography; Bermondsey and Southwark have river frontages along the Thames. They were working-class areas with industry, which was manned by many local people from tenement buildings and houses in crowded little streets.

Bermondsey still has fine examples of the pre-war estates and dockers' cottages in the vicinity of Surrey Docks. The docks dominated pre- and post-war industry in the Rotherhithe part of Bermondsey. Surrey Docks were renowned for importing timber from across the globe, particularly from Scandinavia and Canada, along with grain and foodstuffs. There are still Scandinavian churches near the entrance to the Rotherhithe Tunnel for foreign seamen to worship in. Particularly dominant is the Norwegian church on the roundabout by the entrance to the tunnel. Broadcasts by the BBC were made to celebrate Norwegian Independence Day as this was forbidden in Norway by the occupying Germans.

Bermondsey was also known worldwide for its leather and fur and industries, some of which contributed to the war effort. The sheepskin linings for RAF pilots' jackets were fashioned at the C. W. Martin's Alaska Factory housed in Grange Road. This is now an apartment block but still retains its beautiful art deco exterior. Barrow Hepburn and Gale made leather belts for the military in their premises in Grange Walk. Again, the area was surrounded by tenement blocks that supplied much of the labour force to the local industries of the day.

Southwark was well known for 'hops and hats', as a fellow historian once described it. Indeed, the famous bowler had its birth in Southwark Bridge Road. There is still much evidence of the brewing trade, including the beautiful Hop Exchange building in Southwark Street. I can remember the Courage Brewery building in the early 1980s as my train to work chugged round from London Bridge to Cannon Street. Now, the area around Southwark Cathedral is a maze of offices, wine bars and bistros. Much of the area has been redefined as Crossrail approaches.

The river front was dominated by wharfs and warehouses. Just to the east of London Bridge is Hays Wharf, once known as 'London's Larder'. The area running between Southwark Street and Union Street was home to much small and light industry; Charles Letts, the diary producers, had their home in the vicinity as did Wilcox's Engineering Company. A browse though the commercial section of the pre-war Post Office directories bears testament to this busy warren of enterprise. As with Bermondsey, local social housing provided the backbone of the workforce. The Tate Modern along Southwark's river frontage was formerly the Bankside Power Station, a big target for the Luftwaffe, as was the Blackfriars Railway Goods Yard running parallel to Blackfriars Road just south of the Thames.

The Elephant and Castle roundabout, currently going through a very large makeover, was a very vital target for the Luftwaffe; it was the start of the A2 and A3 main roads. It also had, and still does have, roads leading to important Thames bridges: London Bridge, Southwark Bridge, Blackfriars Bridge and Waterloo Bridge – all part of the lifeblood for wartime London.

Camberwell has many more open spaces than its aforementioned neighbours: Dulwich Park, Peckham Rye, Dulwich and Sydenham Golf Club and a variety of sports clubs on its southern border with Lambeth. There are also the two famous public schools, Dulwich College and Alleyn's, both with vast acres of grounds. However, being such a large borough it had its own diversity within. The working-class districts were apparent on the east of the borough, where Peckham meets Bermondsey, in particular where the South-East Metropolitan Gas Works were located in the Old Kent Road. Coming almost west from this spot, the visitor encounters Burgess Park, now a vast open space with modern facilities, but was once home to light and medium industry surrounded by the homes of its workers. Modern estates now sprawl across to Rye Lane, Peckham, a major high street for shoppers.

South of Rye Lane lies Peckham Rye, a vast open expanse of park land where football and cricket matches are in abundance during their respective seasons. During the Second World War, the Rye had a different role; it was a prisoner-of-war camp for captured service personnel. The girls from nearby Honor Oak Girls' School were banned from the Rye as a friendly snowball fight with some Italian prisoners was seen as 'fraternization with the enemy' by the local police.

Camberwell boasts three cemeteries. There is the Camberwell Old Cemetery in Forest Hill Road, which houses Victorian and modern graves along with a First World War Heroes' Corner. Nearby Brenchley Gardens is Camberwell New Cemetery, which as the name suggests is for more recent deaths. Again, it has a Heroes' Corner (for the Second World War) as well as a memorial to the civilian war dead of from Bermondsey, Camberwell and Southwark who are buried or were cremated there.

The third cemetery in modern Southwark is better known than its counterparts. Nunhead Cemetery is one of London's 'Magnificent Seven' cemeteries. As with Camberwell New Cemetery, civilian war dead are buried here as well as First and Second World War service personnel. The cemetery was hit many times in the Blitz; its shattered graves complement its Gothic splendour.

The writing of this book has been an incredible journey of discovery, of tales of bravery and self-sacrifice by ordinary people. Exploring the streets of modern Southwark in the late summer and early autumn looking for evidence and new tales was extremely rewarding.

The writing of the book wouldn't have been possible without the enormous help, encouragement and friendship of the following people.

I would like to thank my dear friend Marietta Crichton-Stuart, who provided so much of the background for the book and often joined me in traipsing the streets on a Sunday morning, and John Terry, who has been a wonderful source of information and encouragement.I would also like to thank Ray Stroud, Henry Varley, Harry Winter, the Lakin Family, Germander Speedwell, Mick Reardon, Gary Magold, Maurice Klingels, Richard Clarke, Owen Sheppard of *Southwark News*, Mark Parker, Tony Budgen, Dawn Monks and finally Bob Hobbs for putting up with my ramblings of new stories and discoveries. I am grateful to the Dulwich and Sydenham Golf Club; St Katherine's Church, Eugenia Road; St John's Church, East Dulwich and the Friends of Southwark Park.

A big thank you, also, to Dr Patricia Dark, Lucy Tann and Lisa Soverall of the Southwark Local Studies Library for their great help and patience and for providing some of the photographs.

I would finally like to thank my lovely wife Tracey for all her help, support and love with every project I undertake.

The Build-up to the Blitz

Hitler's aggressive expansionist policy unfolded with the annexation of his native Austria in 1938 and Czechoslovakia the same year. British Prime Minister Neville Chamberlain flew out to Munich to meet with the Germans, returning to the UK, brandishing the infamous piece of paper that promised 'peace in our time' – not a sentiment entirely shared by the population.

Local authorities, who were responsible for their own civil defence arrangements, were busily making plans for the eventuality of war with Germany and the bombing of the masses by air. Other institutions followed suit. The St Paul's cathedral spring meeting of 1938 was dominated by the concern of the protection of the cathedral in the event of London being bombed and the idea of the 'St Paul's Watch' was hatched.

The London Borough of Islington delivered Anderson shelters to some of its population as early as February 1939; admittedly, space was running out in the depot where these were stored. The Borough of Camberwell followed suit in the March. Bermondsey boasted it could provide shelter for 55,000 persons and was christened in the press, 'The London Borough of Shelter'.

Further plans to expand German control turned eastwards. A secret non-aggression pact was shaped between Germany and Russia; the sting in the tail was for the two countries to attack and carve up Poland. With Britain and France guaranteeing to come to Poland's aid should there be an attack, Hitler needed a dormant Russia while he dealt with Britain and France. As history reminds us, it was Hitler's intention to attack and invade Russia once his western flank in Europe was secure.

German troops marched into Poland on 1 September 1939. Britain issued an ultimatum to Germany for the withdrawal of German troops on 3 September. No response came from the German Embassy in London and no withdrawal was forthcoming. Consequently at 11 a.m. on 3 September, Chamberlain announced to the country that Britain was at war with Germany. The French also declared war with Germany a short time after Chamberlain's announcement. Ironically, the air-raid sirens in London sounded almost immediately following the declaration of war; this alert was caused by the untimely arrival of a French military aircraft over these shores.

The outbreak of war sprung the mass evacuation of children and some mothers to the safety of rural towns and villages. For a further insight into the evacuation and the plight of the evacuees, Mike Brown's excellent series of Home Front books are recommended.

A blackout was enforced across the nation with stiff penalties for a breach in these laws. Air Raid Wardens were now on their beats enforcing these measures.

However, the period following the outbreak of war was something of an anticlimax; with little happening on the military front, the period became known as the 'Phoney War'. The wardens were becoming increasingly unpopular with local populations, being treated as 'busybodies'. When the Blitz finally came, as this book will show, the Wardens' Service and other Civil Defence Services put their lives on the line, showing the utmost bravery in many intense and dangerous situations.

As previously stated, Britain was gearing up for the possibility war from 1938. It was realised that if cities were to be bombed and mass fires were the result, the National Fire Service (NFS) was too small to deal with the situation. Therefore, the Auxiliary Fire Service (AFS) was conceived. They had no regular fire equipment; in many cases their 'fire engine' was a London taxi with their equipment stored on a trailer behind. Often their 'fire stations' were schoolyards and garage premises. The wage was £3 10s per week (less for female personnel), and they were exempt from military call-up. Like the Wardens' Service, these fire personnel were much maligned particularly during the Phoney War as there was little for them to do in this period. Comments such as 'You get £3 10/- a week to play darts!' were abundant. As the Blitz unfolded, these brave people came to the fore. A visit to the firefighters' memorial in Godliman Street, situated in the shadow of St Paul's Cathedral, will testify to their bravery and endurance. Many of these auxiliaries joined because they would not take a life, but would put their own life on the line to save others.

A chilling statistic was that only 20 per cent of the auxiliaries had fought a fire by the time the Blitz arrived. However, the auxiliaries from the station in Southwark Bridge Road were in attendance at a fire in C. W. Martin's fur factory in Grange Road, Bermondsey, in early 1940 when some beaver pelts caught fire due to an electrical fault.

Germany was not blessed with natural resources and relied on neutral Sweden for certain imports. To protect the supply routes from Sweden to the Fatherland, neutral Denmark and Norway were invaded on 9 April 1940. Britain and France sent a force to Norway but this attack could not be sustained, the Allied forces returning in defeat.

Following the successes in Eastern Europe it was now the time for Germany's invasion of Western Europe, which was launched on 10 May 1940. Since September 1939, Britain had an Expeditionary Force (BEF) in France, the figure reaching over 300,000 by March 1940.

The German attacks and the speed of the attacks caught the Allies by surprise, particularly the 'right hook' through the Ardennes sweeping up to the Channel ports and threatening to cut off the BEF. As the Germans swept through Holland, Belgium and France the only tangible option for the BEF was to try and make the Channel ports for possible evacuation. The German Army, supported by the Luftwaffe, were all-conquering, and there was very little the Allies could do about it.

Operation Dynamo, now so famous in the annals of history, was the plan to bring as many of the BEF back to the UK as possible. The evacuation of France and Belgium was launched on 26 May 1940 under the command of Admiral Bertram Ramsay and lasted until 4 June 1940. As an aside, British troops were still landing in northern France as the evacuation unfolded; such was the confusion.

Vast amounts of arms and equipment were left behind, spiked or immobilised where possible, but many thousands of Allied troops were brought back to these shores in 'the Miracle of Dunkirk'. It is well documented how the armada of 'Little Ships' assisted the incredible work of the Royal and merchant navies.

In the meantime, Italy had declared war on Britain and France. Also during June 1940, Russia gobbled up Lithuania, Latvia and Estonia along with parts of eastern Romania.

With the capitulation of the Low Countries, France finally surrendered on 14 June 1940. The ultimate insult to Allied victory in the First World War, on Hitler's orders, was the blowing up of the railway carriage in Paris where the Germans had surrendered in 1918.

Britain now stood alone against Hitler, the master of Europe. His natural resources were secure to the north, and the oil fields of captured southern Europe would fire the engines of the German battlewagons.

Hitler was now prepared for the invasion of Britain, but a combination of factors made this impossible despite the relative ease in the defeat of the Allies on the Continent. Twenty-two miles of the English Channel was the problem. Invasion barges were being stacked up in the Channel ports in France and Belgium. The Royal Navy would be the ultimate threat to these. Therefore, the Germans were aware that and Royal Air Force would have to be defeated as it would protect the Navy.

British Fighter Command was smaller in number to its German combatants, and the Luftwaffe had gained experience in Spain, Poland, France and the Low Countries. A small body of British pilots had a little experience over the skies of Dunkirk.

From occupied France, Germany was able to occupy the Channel Islands on 1 July, just sitting a few miles of the French coast.

Phase 1 of the Battle of Britain was about to unfold. On 10 July, the Luftwaffe started to raid British convoys in the Channel, the idea being to tease Fighter

Command into battle. The idea was twofold – to wear down the resources of Fighter Command and to give their own pilots further combat experience.

Minelaying in the Channel and around the coast started in the July – again, a move to make supplying an island nation more difficult and hazardous.

In Phase 2 of the Battle of Britain, Germany started their campaign of bombing coastal airfields and forward landing grounds. Radar stations had been targeted several days earlier. Attacks on airfields further inland followed as the week progressed.

15 August became known as 'Black Thursday' for the Luftwaffe as it lost seventy-five planes that day with Fighter Command losing less than half of that number.

18 August was the 'Hardest Day' with intense aerial combat. The airfields in the south and south-east of England were bombed and, in RAF Kenley's case, mauled. However, Reichsmarschall Hermann Goering was not delivering his earlier boast to Hitler that he could defeat the RAF to pave the way for invasion.

It was still not Hitler's intention to bomb London. From the relatively safe streets of south London it is not difficult to imagine young boys marvelling at the thrills and spills of the dogfights going on a few miles away over the skies of north Kent and Surrey.

The Germans changed tactics slightly and began to bomb British aircraft production on the 19th with a switch back to the airfields on the 23rd.

Targets were now also industrial, such as oil refineries, like Thameshaven on the Thames Estuary. Suburbs of London by now had also been hit, but still there was no directive from Hitler to bomb London.

In bad weather on the 24th, the crew of a Luftwaffe bomber thought they were over Thameshaven and jettisoned their bombs. This action changed the course of the war and the history of London. The bombs hit Fore Street in the City of London, near the Barbican. As a reprisal the RAF bombed Berlin. An incensed Hitler changed his tactics, ordering the first mass attack on London on 7 September 1940.

It is here that Bermondsey, Southwark and Camberwell's story begins as they faced several stages of the Blitz.

Abbey Furnishing Stores, Abbey Street, in readiness for the air raids. (Southwark Local Studies Library)

Air-raid shelter sign on the Lockyer Estate. (Author's collection)

BERMONDSEY CIVIL DEFENCE

Use your Shelter Quietly and Regularly.

KEEP IT TIDY AND CLEAN.

Shelter Licences will be Withdrawn or Cancelled if at any time ANY of the following things happen:

HOLDER DISREGARDS ORDER OF **MARSHAL**, POLICEMAN OR AUTHORISED OFFICIAL.

EARNS THE DISPLEASURE OF OTHERS BY ALLOWING A MEMBER OF HIS FAMILY TO COMMIT ANY OFFENCE, NUISANCE OR DISTURBANCE, OR FAILS TO KEEP THE SHELTER TIDY AND CLEAN.

LEAVES THE BUNK FOR FOUR NIGHTS WITHOUT NOTICE TO MARSHAL.

TRANSFERS THIS LICENCE TO ANOTHER PERSON.

ENGAGES IN **GAMBLING**.

REFUSES TO REMOVE BEDDING & BELONGINGS FOR SHELTER CLEANSING PURPOSES.

Bermondsey air-raid shelter poster. (Southwark Local Studies Library)

The quaint former Peter Hills School was used as accommodation for Auxiliary Fire Service personnel. (Author's collection)

The Washing Service provides much assistance to those bombed out of East Surrey Grove. (Southwark Local Studies Library)

Camberwell Civil Defence Service provide firefighting training. (Southwark Local Studies Library)

METROPOLITAN BOROUGH OF SOUTHWARK
AIR RAID PRECAUTIONS
ENROLMENT OFFICES

Volunteers for Air Raid Precautions may enrol at the following Offices:

	TOWN HALL Walworth Rd., S.E.17	BROWNING INSTITUTE Walworth Rd., S.E.17	WOMEN'S VOLUNTARY SERVICES 127 Walworth Rd., S.E.17
MONDAYS	9.30 a.m.—7.30 p.m.	9.0 a.m.—7.30 p.m.	12.30 p.m.—8.30 p.m.
TUESDAYS	,, 5.30 ,,	,, 5. 0 ,,	,, ,,
WEDNESDAYS	,, 7.30 ,,	,, 7.30 ,,	,, ,,
THURSDAYS	,, 5.30 ,,	,, 5. 0 ,,	,, ,,
FRIDAYS	,, 5.30 ,,	,, 5. 0 ,,	,, ,,
SATURDAYS	,, 1. 0 ,,	,, 1. 0 ,,	,, 5. 0 p.m.

A letter addressed to either of these offices, will receive immediate attention

D. T. GRIFFITHS
Town Clerk, Air Raid Precautions Officer

Wightman & Co. Ltd. R 9742

Above: Southwark Council ARP recruitment poster. (Southwark Local Studies Library)

Opposite: A bollard in Southwark Bridge Road still displaying its blackout paint. (Author's collection)

Church prayer cards that were left over from the First World War were used again in the Second World War to send prayers to loved ones fighting overseas. (Southwark Local Studies Library)

1940
The Blitz Cometh

In September 1927, Dr Alfred Salter, Bermondsey's pacifist MP, had a premonition that should there be another war, Bermondsey will be an area of smashed buildings, wrecked factories, devastated houses, mangled corpses and bodies of helpless men, women and children writhing and suffocating under clouds of gas fumes.

His prophecy came true with the exception of the gas fumes.

The official date for the start of the Night Blitz is 7 September 1940. However, bombs were dropping on the capital prior to this date and, needless to say, there were casualties.

The first person to be killed in Bermondsey was when a bomb landed on a house in Storks Road, the home of Sarah Hough. She was rushed to St Olave's Hospital but failed to survive. The same night, two high-explosive bombs penetrated the railway over the Linsey Street Arch air-raid shelter and five shelterers were killed.

In Southwark the Blitz came early for its residents. Just off the Old Kent Road near the Bricklayer's Arms was Arnott Street – a small street of terraced houses, home to a tight-knit and friendly community.

Death had already hit the residents of Arnott Street when 'one of their own', Edward Saunders, was killed on 16 August while serving with the RAF. He is buried in Nunhead Cemetery. Edward attended the local school at the end of the street, Joseph Lancaster, and as his coffin was brought from his mother's house for the funeral many school children from the school adorned the street with their heads bowed. Edward was the son of Mary Saunders of No. 72.

On 6 September 1940 at 11.44 p.m., just as the residents of the street were checking their blackout curtains, preparing for bed and looking forward to another sunny weekend, a high-explosive bomb smashed and exploded in the street. Sophie Hatton recalled,

Just as we got back into bed the sirens sounded. I got to the top of the stairs then suddenly before I realised what had happened I was blown all the way to the bottom. I rushed for the dug-out and as I got there bricks and stuff fell on it.

Twelve people were killed that night in Arnott Street, including five members of the North family and three members of the Dunkley family.

Annie Leary was paralysed in the legs from the blast. Some weeks later in an interview with the *Daily Express*, the sixty-six-year-old said, 'Hitler can't break a Cockney's Heart!'[i]

Sadly, Arnott Street is no longer there. The Blitz could not break the street's heart, but in a familiar story it fell prey to development and the expansion of the school.

Several days earlier, on 29 August, a twist of irony had occurred. On the very tip of where Camberwell meets Lambeth at West Dulwich, a high-explosive bomb landed near No. 7 Allison Grove, the home of the parents of William Joyce, 'Lord Haw-Haw', the traitor who became the voice of the radio broadcasts from Berlin, *Germany Calling*. Mr and Mrs Joyce, who had been sheltering in the basement, were shaken up but uninjured.

No deaths were recorded in Camberwell prior to 7 September. Of the seventeen incidents recorded in the Wardens' log, ten were high-explosive bombs, some unexploded, with several falling on open ground.

Saturday 7 September 1940 was a lovely late summer, early autumn day. The menfolk of south-east London were eagerly awaiting the local football derby, Millwall versus Charlton, at the Den in New Cross.

Alan Tizzard was a local Rotherhithe boy. He recalls 7 September vividly as follows.

On that sunny summer afternoon I was sitting on the kitchen step whittling away at my model when the sirens sounded. No sooner had the sirens sounded than planes came into sight. They were high by the standards of the day, maybe 20,000 feet. They were twisting and turning, bobbing and weaving. To me this was a grand show. So far my sight of war had been at a distance and this knocked the cinema into a cocked hat.

From the front of the house we did not see the approach of part of Luftwaffe Zwei; from across the Channel they came in from behind us. A sudden shower of spent cartridge cases rained down all around us. What had been the dull ever-changing drone of the fighters in dogfights high above our heads with their guns making no more than a phut changed to pandemonium. The stakes had changed. We were now part of it.[ii]

Alan was witnessing the start of the Night Blitz.

At 4.35 p.m., around 350 German aircraft made their way up the Thames Estuary towards London. Their main targets were the docks on both sides of the river, the Woolwich Arsenal, West Ham Power Station and Beckton Gas Works.

In the clear light of the afternoon, the bombers had no difficulty in locating their targets. First to be hit was Ford's motor plant at Dagenham, quickly followed by Beckton Gas Works. The Royal Docks were also an easy target and these were struck with ferocity along with the vessels moored alongside.

The East End of London was devastated. All types of dockside warehouses and factories were ablaze, along with the homes of the local population. The River Fire Service had a desperate task as burning barges and small craft drifted aimlessly along the river, posing a deadly threat to the boats and crews.

At 7.30 p.m. the Luftwaffe were back to drop more bombs into the fires of London, now blazing out of control.

With the deadly work done, the Luftwaffe returned to their continental bases as dawn approached on 8 September. This was to be the start of bombing for fifty-seven nights of the most famous city in the world.

At approximately 6 p.m. the first bombs started landing in Bermondsey; Southwark appeared to have been largely bypassed in this first raid with a small amount of incendiary bombs falling. Deputy Warden Pullen of Wardens' Post 12 in Amelia Street recalled that his wardens were ready for action on the west side of Walworth Road, but the raiders withdrew with British fighters hot on their tail. He remembers the all-clear sounding and his wardens going home.[iii]

Camberwell got its fair share of attention from the Luftwaffe in this initial raid, one of the targets being the South-East Metropolitan Gas Works in the Old Kent Road, very close to the boundary with Camberwell.

With the destruction of London's docks a high priority for the Luftwaffe on that day, Surrey Docks was always going to be a main target and nearly became a death trap for its residents. There were only two roads in and out of the Surrey Docks peninsula: Redriff Road, which led to the area known as 'Downtown' in the eastern side of the docks, and Brunel Road on the western side.

With the bombs starting fall into the wood yards and the streets of dockers' cottages and flats, the residents were clearly in trouble. With the ferocity of the raid and the heat, both roads buckled and were virtually impassable. The NFS and AFS from all parts of London and the home counties were in attendance at the docks, fighting a losing battle against the flames, but the people from 'Downtown' had to be got out to relative safety. In the flats the wind was whipping up a fire storm and destroying everything in its path.

It is at times like these, when all seems lost that heroes and heroines emerge. Grace Rattenbury was a charity worker working for the Women's Voluntary Service. Forty-year-old Grace stepped up to the plate and volunteered to drive her WVS van into the inferno of the docks and bring as many people as she could in a shuttle service to Keetons Road Rest Centre, a few hundred yards away just off Jamaica Road.

Time and time again she had to duck down in her van as more bombs were falling, the van becoming blistered through the intense heat. She had to dodge bomb craters that she could hardly see through the fog-like smoke of the burning wood piles.

Many people owed their lives to Grace's bravery, but there was a cruel twist of fate to follow in the early hours of the following morning.

One of those instrumental in the evacuation of Surrey Docks, was John 'Joe' Blake, the liaison officer to Bermondsey Civil Defence Services. He was in the Rotherhithe Street area of 'Downtown'. When his work was finished there, Joe returned to the control room at the Town Hall. He reported that there was terrible havoc caused by fire and bombs and that on numerous instances the evacuees fell flat on their stomachs time and time again to dodge the bombs.

Thomas Winter lived in 'Downtown' with his family. His mother had gone off to do the usual Saturday shop. She left clear instructions that should the air-raid siren sound, Thomas and his siblings should head for the shelter. As the siren wailed later in the afternoon, off they went, as instructed, to the community shelter in the corner of the block where they lived.

As the raid unfolded, the noise of the bombs thundering to earth, combined with the noise from the anti-aircraft guns in Southwark Park and across the river on the Isle of Dogs, was incredible. Bombs landing close by shook the shelter, and Thomas thought it was only a matter of time before the shelter took a direct hit and death was upon them. News got back to the shelter that Surrey Docks were now a blazing inferno. The situation in the shelter was becoming untenable, and evacuation was the only course.

As they left the shelter, Thomas said the whole area was an orange glow and the smoke from the fires made it nearly impossible to breathe. Their escape route would be along Bryan Road past Holy Trinity church, but the pavement was a mass of twisted concrete. Firefighters came up with the answer – an arch of water from their hoses against the wall of Holy Trinity through which 200 shelterers escaped.

It was mooted to take them across to the Isle of Dogs by boat, but that idea went awry as the jetty on the river bank began to collapse. So along Rotherhithe Street they tramped and finally met up with their father; he had been helping others escape. He told them to head for Keetons Road Rest Centre where they would be warm and safe.

They reached the junction of Jamaica Road and Southwark Park Road when family friend Mary Elliott spotted the family. She insisted they come with her and they ended up at the John Bull Arch Shelter in the Blue Anchor just in time as the second wave of bombers was about to unleash their deadly payload upon London. Little did they know it but the Winter family had their second lucky escape that day.[iv]

One of the last boats to get away to the relative safety of the Isle of Dogs was brought in by Thames lighterman James Bowtell. With great skill and aplomb, he successfully navigated through fifty dumbbarges that were adrift in the river, some alight. With bombs still falling in the area, he and his crew brought fifty people across the river from South Dock.

Some of the staff of the Smallpox Isolation Centre at South Wharf, along with local residents, were in peril. William Petley was a fifty-nine-year-old local council mechanic and First World War veteran who had been mentioned in dispatches. He was instrumental in the helping with the evacuation and attempting to fight fires. He remained in the vicinity until the evacuation was complete.

Samuel Melvin was a riverboat fireman. He had just cycled home from his afternoon shift to his home in Peckham when a neighbour told him Surrey Docks were on fire. Bidding his wife goodbye at the door he cycled back with all haste, but found no fire boat crew at his substation; they were all out on the river, using its water to tackle the ever increasing flames.

In the watchroom he came across Lewisham fireman Tim Muir and six other firemen at South Dock. Muir told Melvin that everyone had been taken away by boats. They decided to tackle the blaze at South Wharf. Finding a Dennis trailer pump unattended, the scratch crew tried to tackle the blaze on a row of cottages and damp down a block of flats that was in danger of burning.

It was discovered that there was one person still in the Smallpox Isolation Centre – Sister Hope, the matron of the centre. Melvin and Muir succeeded in rescuing her from the now-blazing building.

They were fighting a losing battle against the ever-increasing inferno; it was decided to look for a way out. All the firemen and the matron clambered into a fire tender and gingerly tried to drive their way out. Melvin was at the wheel. The dense smoke made it virtually impossible to see where they were going. All of a sudden the fire tender plunged into a bomb crater full of water. They all scrambled out safely. Fortunately, an abandoned car was close at hand, but there was no key in the ignition. Searching desperately, Melvin found a deserted AFS taxi and in they piled. The journey was a nightmare; the windows were too hot to touch in the searing heat. Their nightmare ended as they reached Cherry Garden Street and away from the inferno that was Surrey Docks.

Rescue party worker William Austin was returning with his colleagues after a rescue in Redriff Road; they were driving along Southwark Park Road back to Bermondsey Town Hall Control Centre to pick up fresh orders. Hearing the wail of a bomb, the driver quickly pulled over and the rescue party all dived under it for cover. They were covered in debris as the bomb had dropped on an abandoned picture house at the junction with Ambrose Street. After a search for any occupants, it was agreed that the building was empty.

Suddenly screams were heard along the road; an oil bomb had hit an Anderson Shelter further along Ambrose Street, setting the shelter and house on fire. William Austin was away like a shot towards the centre of the blaze, the Anderson Shelter. Defying the flames and intense heat, he managed to evacuate five people alive from the inferno. Austin collapsed from his exertions and had to be carried back the lorry.

Air-raid shelters were soon to become a way of life for the beleaguered residents of London, whether it was in their own Anderson shelters, large and small communal shelters in warehouses or under blocks of flats. Doris Datchler remembered her days in the shelter of the basement in the Pembroke College Mission.

> When the raids started in September 1940, we all used to go downstairs to the Pembroke College Mission. There we sat on long seats; mums, dads, kids and grans. My old dad, Ted French, would come down with a big basket of crab legs that he would distribute to as many people as he was able. Anyone who was lucky enough to get one would call out, 'Anyone got a hairpin they don't want?' (to get the crab meat out).[v]

While the emergency services were being tested to the limit in Bermondsey, things were tough too in Camberwell. A solitary high-explosive bomb fell on a connecting bridge at the South-East London Metropolitan Gas Works and exploded, making a small crater. Fortunately, the Home Guard and local workmen were quickly on the spot to ensure no fire broke out.

Sandgate Street is tucked in behind the South-East Metropolitan Gas Works. It is now primarily populated by warehouses and depots. Back in 1940, it was dominated by houses. Numbers 30 and 32 took a direct hit, killing occupants Annie and James Colegate, plus four members of the Lucas family.

Things were no better on the southern side of the Old Kent Road; not far away from Sandgate Street is Green Hundred Road; Northfield House was hit, killing four people in the block.

Southwark fared much better than Bermondsey and Camberwell, being further west. Incendiary bombs were largely the culprits on 7 September. Manor Place bore the brunt of these with wardens from Post 12 quickly putting out the fires. As Deputy Warden Pullen looked eastwards, he was concerned about the glow in the sky. 'As the shadows of night began to fall; by dusk the sky was a bright orange glare.'[vi]

Just before midnight at Keetons Road Rest Centre, a school in peace time, people evacuated from 'Downtown' were warm and dry, had eaten and were settling in for the night following their afternoon and evening ordeal. At one minute past midnight all hell broke loose as a high-explosive bomb found its mark at the rear of the school followed by another a few minutes later.

Joan Creed was working as a clerical assistant at the rest centre for the L. C. C. social welfare department. Joan and colleagues were marshalling new arrivals and helping them settle in. The shelter at the rear of the centre was crammed with evacuees. The centre staff were not exempt from the blast of the bomb – Mr Attwood, Mr Ost, Mr Bennett and Joan were hit by shrapnel; Mr Gale had an injured foot; but Mr Montgomerie, suffering from shock, was immediately dispatched to hospital. Shelter helper Robert Marshall was killed instantly.

All of the centre staff carried on as best they could, tending to the wounded and evacuating people from the site. Attwood and Bennett did the best they could, but their injuries got the better of them and they had to stand down. Ost was partially blinded; holding his eyes, he wanted to carry on but was persuaded to stand down too.

Joan picked herself up from the first blast and started stretcher work with the aid of a soldier. The second blast threw them both off their feet with the soldier landing on top of Joan, but they manfully carried on. Joan then changed roles, acting as an ambulance attendant. After several trips to St Olave's Hospital, it was noticed that Joan was bleeding badly from her shrapnel wounds in the leg. By 4 a.m. she was receiving treatment at a first aid post but reported to her office for duty several hours later.

I was asked to provide a private walk for a family around Bermondsey in the summer of 2015 with a particular emphasis on Keetons Road and a casualty from Acorn Walk, Annie Lakin. The father, Roy, was in his mid-seventies. As we approached the site of where the school was, Roy said to me, 'I was probably here, you know? I was two years of age and don't remember it. My mother was Annie Lakin.' I left the family on the spot for five minutes with their thoughts. A stiff drink was required as we took a break in the walk at the father's request. I will never forget that day. Annie Lakin was one of thirty-nine people who lost their lives at Keetons Road rest centre.

At 1 a.m. on 8 September Joe Blake was restless. He had heard that a fireman was wounded somewhere on the docks. Joe was given permission to go and investigate. As he drove along Redriff Road, properties on either side of the road were still ablaze. As he proceeded with caution a bomb exploded in front of the car, wrecking it. Joe had to proceed on foot and got into the dock complex through a hole in the fence.

After a time Joe found six seriously wounded firemen who would require transportation to hospital as soon as possible. He found a phone in Rotherhithe Street and telephoned the control centre to get the ambulance dispatched. Two high-explosive bombs fell very close, and Joe was blown away from the apparatus. His first comment to Bermondsey Control when he recovered his posture was 'Blimey, that was ruddy close!'

The ambulance duly arrived, but sadly firemen Harry Marshall and Richard Martin succumbed to their wounds; however, Joe's brave and prompt actions did save some lives.

A further legacy of the night of 7/8 September 1940 was when an incendiary bomb fell in Arnside Street, Walworth. It landed on a storage building of the Records Office, now known as the National Archives. Here was stored the First World War service papers of the ordinary ranks of the British Army. The Fire Service was unable to get water to the stricken building. Fires spread along Merrow Street towards the shops in Walworth Road. It is estimated that around 70 per cent of these service records were lost – a real loss for many generations of family and military historians.

So ended the first concentrated attack on London, leaving the East End and parts of south-east London devastated. This was the start of the Night Blitz, and London and its people were to suffer more.

Horrified by the events at Keetons Road School, the king made a visit the following day and was visibly moved. He spoke to the school caretaker, Mr Miles and his family. Miles recalled,

The King spoke to me as man to man. You could see how shocked he was by the damage. He was kind and had a warm feeling for ordinary people no matter how humble. And I shall never forget the pain and suffering in his face when he caught sight of the bodies of the raid victims among the debris.[vii]

The Luftwaffe was back the following day, 8 September, with a morning raid along the Isle of Sheppey and up the Thames Estuary. London was attacked from 7.30 p.m., the attack lasting through till 5 a.m. the following morning.

On 8 September, a *South London Press* reporter visited Surrey Docks. He found a scene of utter devastation; smashed houses had crumbled on to broken roads. Holy Trinity Church in Bryan Road was just a mass of fire-scarred bricks; everything combustible such as hymn books, alters and prayer kneelers were no more, and 1.5 million tons of wood that had been in storage had gone up in smoke with the charred remnants smouldering away. Bermondsey police stations were inundated with locals frantically seeking news of their loved ones.

Some of the residents had filtered back to site of their former homes, pathetically seeking to salvage something, anything that may be a family memory or something of value.

Despite the Luftwaffe's return, the casualties in Bermondsey were not as heavy in comparison to the previous day. On the night of 8/9 September, the Royal Oak public house in Maltby Street took a direct hit, killing local resident Bayliss Swann, landlady Esther Thompson and her seventeen-year-old son Henry. Bayliss Swann's widow, Rose, was to have further grief bestowed on her later in the Blitz.

Incendiary bombs were particularly prevalent across Camberwell, with many properties in the borough succumbing to fires.

9 September brought one of Camberwell's most tragic incidents. Local residents were sheltering in No. 5 shelter under Wheatland House on the Dog Kennel Hill Estate when the block took a direct hit from a high-explosive bomb. The scene was appalling. Local volunteer warden Ernest Ash set about rescuing some of those trapped. He entered the wrecked shelter on several occasions, often becoming trapped himself by falling debris and masonry. He held up parts of the structure, allowing colleagues, P. V. Davis and A. Bonsor to bring people out. The rescue was even more remarkable as the raid was still in progress and a neighbouring block was on fire from a hit by an oil bomb.

Despite the valiant efforts of the Wardens' service, twenty-nine people lost their lives. Local opinion was that the almost-square blocks of flats potentially looked like army barracks and the estate seemed to attract the Luftwaffe's attention an unerring number of times.

In the early hours of 10 September, it was Southwark's turn to experience a major incident. Ewer Street is small cut-through from Union Street almost up to Southwark Street. At the Southwark Street end was a public bathhouse with a communal shelter next to it. Most of the shelterers were from the Guinness Trust flats in Union Street, most residents preferring Ewer Street and the deep shelter at the borough to the shelters provided by their landlords. Tragedy struck at 3.20 a.m. as a high-explosive bomb scored a direct hit on the shelter. The nearby railway arch was damaged, the gas main was severed and fire raged. Seventeen people were directly killed in the shelter with one further casualty, Lottie Hackett succumbing to her injuries a day later in Guy's Hospital.

Mr J. Hunt lived in Crewys Road, Nunhead, and recalls 11 September in his part of Camberwell:

> Very near to us was a large block of back-to-back terraced houses situated between Lugard Road, BrayardsRoad and Hollydale Road. We heard a tremendous explosion one night and heard the following day that half a large block had been reduced to rubble by just one bomb. My friends and I went to look at the damage and saw, what I firmly believe to this day, to have been a large heap of human intestines. We were hurried away by an Air Raid Warden before we could get too close.[viii]

Fifty-seven-year old Camberwell resident, Amy Fluck, ran an all-night coffee stall in the Old Kent Road, the stall being situated just in neighbouring Lewisham. She supplied food and beverages to local civil defence personnel and munitions workers. 'Bubbles', as she was affectionately known, kept her stall open without fail seven nights per week.

A big fire was raging on 11 September, and 'Bubbles' was supplying hot tea to the attendant firefighters. Suddenly an anti-aircraft shell exploded close to her stall; Amy was badly wounded in the thigh and was rushed to St Giles' Hospital by ambulance. The journey to the hospital was fraught with danger as a raid was still in progress. The ambulance had to crash through a wall of flames, and Cyril, Amy's husband, was quick to praise the skill and bravery of the driver.

Amy insisted that Cyril place a Union Jack on the coffee stall adorned with the words, 'Ceased but not subdued (got that Adolph!), open in a couple of days'.

Amy was moved to several hospitals outside London. On 7 October, Cyril was visiting Amy in the evening when a high explosive thundered into the hospital. Cyril was pinned up against a wall with a beam in his back. He managed to shake himself free and crawl under Amy's bed and then to safety. Despite being freed by the rescue services, Amy did not survive. She is recorded as a Sutton casualty, but she was one of 'south London's own'.[ix]

Camberwell got a considerable peppering on 11 September, particularly the area to the west of Rye Lane and Nunhead. Section Officer George Nicholls, a local fireman, effected a difficult and dangerous rescue of a woman in a bombed house in Anstey Road, the roof collapsing shortly after he got the woman out. Fifteen people were killed in Camberwell, including a two-year-old and a five-year-old in Surrey Road.

A small lull came for Bermondsey with fewer bombs falling than since the start of the Blitz with only one person recorded as dying in the borough in three days. Southwark was not as lucky on 12 September as the areas either side of Walworth Road received particular attention from the Luftwaffe. Just off of East Street, the Orb Street shelter took a direct hit; neighbouring streets were also hit, more than likely by the same stick of bombs. Thirty-three people were killed, most of them in the shelter. The three Fozzard children had their own shelter at the family home in Nursery Row, their parents having a separate shelter. The three children, David, Florence and Joseph were all killed while grief-stricken parents Ernest and Mary survived.

15 September 1940 was a red-letter day in the Blitz. The Luftwaffe was now not going to win the Battle of Britain, and there would be no invasion in 1940. Fighter Command had done its job marvellously and miraculously. With their fighters unable to support their bombers over Britain for more than 10 to 15 minutes, the bombers were exposed to the ever-increasing number of British fighters. The Luftwaffe tactics of day and night bombing changed to one of primarily night bombing. It was a big day in the air with over 600 German aircraft over the United Kingdom during the day.

15 September was the first time in the Blitz that the famous teaching hospital, Guy's, was badly damaged. Sub-officer George Shedden and fireman Frank Arden displayed great courage in fighting their way through the medical block to rescue an injured doctor. The doctor was trapped on the fourth floor. With the main staircase demolished, Shedden and Arden showed great initiative in reaching the doctor, finally effecting the rescue with a lowering line.

Neptune Street, Rotherhithe, had already received its fair share of bombing in the previous week. The street, as its nautical name suggests, is in the shadow of Surrey Docks. At 12.10 a.m. on 16 September a communal shelter took a direct hit. Thirty-five people were in the shelter and were buried under the debris.

On arriving at the scene, rescue party leader Thomas Dunn wasted no time and crawled underneath a precariously balanced portion of the shelter roof to attend to the injured. Dunn and his men, buoyed by his bravery and courage, managed to rescue fifteen people, but another twenty perished.

The shelter at Bermondsey Town Hall in Spa Road took a direct hit from a high-explosive bomb. Among those killed were Commandant Muriel Noel of the Women's Legion, who was in charge of the emergency food supplies, and her assistant, Rebecca Phillips.

17 September was supposed to be the happiest day of Sidney's and Mabel Wright's life. They had married earlier during the day and were enjoying a small reception in the Father Red Cap public house on Camberwell Green. On hearing the air-raid siren, the party reluctantly abandoned the celebrations and took refuge in the shelters on the Green. At 9.35 a.m. a landmine, in use for the first time over London, exploded on the shelter, killing the wedding party of nine and two others.

Another one of the new landmines was responsible for the destruction of properties in Doddington Grove and Cooks Road in the northern part of Southwark on 18 September. Many were trapped and rescue parties worked long and hard to free the victims, but eleven persons perished.

Fort Road, Bermondsey, housed the West Bermondsey Labour Party Institute; next door was a workers' cooperative bakery, the brainchild of Dr Alfred Salter. The buildings were demolished by a landmine that also damaged the Dunton Road police station and a chapel. Fire was also raging. Arthur Foot was the Post Warden for the institute and was trapped in the basement of the building that served as a Wardens' Post. Foot was located ten feet under the debris. As rescue party leader, Ernest Playford, located Foot – a voice yelled that a wall was coming down. Playford quickly made a bridge of his body over Foot's head; Playford was badly injured by falling bricks and masonry. He was immediately removed to the hospital where he remained for some weeks. During the rescue attempt Playford was ably assisted by colleague John Bradley who was also showered with bricks and masonry. Like Playford, he was severely injured and taken to hospital with a broken leg. Arthur Foot sadly died despite the rescue workers' valiant attempts.

First World War veteran Thomas MacFarlane was also during the incident with his stretcher party. Thomas was clearly a man of action, winning the Distinguished Conduct Medal and the Military Medal in that conflict with the Kings Own Scottish Borderers. A small hole was located, big enough for a slim and wiry man to crawl through; Thomas was up for the challenge. He wiggled his way through to where other wardens were trapped and injured. On locating them, he remained with them, administering first aid until their release.

Dustman and Stretcher Party member Edmund Barry was also on the scene. It was learnt that several bakers were trapped in the bakery next door under a 30-ton oven. Edmund tried all he could through the night to rescue the bakers despite being in a precarious position the entire time. His efforts were in vain as Henry Clemence and Arthur Hiom died in the bakery.

All told, eight people died at the incident.

18 September was also the day that the John Lewis department store in Oxford Street was gutted. It was a tough day for London with around 750 people killed or injured.

20 September was a busy day for the firefighters in Bermondsey and Southwark; scores of incendiary bombs were dropped. There were large fires at Sinnot and

Sundt in Druid Street, Scott's Sufferance Wharf and Potty and Co. in Horseleydown Lane. Wardens were also active, dealing with fires in Weston Street. Midwinter's in Southwark Park Road had the top floor burnt out and all the stock was destroyed. St John's Horsleydown Church at the junction of Tower Bridge Road and Fair Street was gutted by a single incendiary bomb. Acting Sub-Officer Sid Baker of the Fire Service showed remarkable devotion to duty while in charge of dealing with the fires in the Dockhead locality. He was hit by an appliance that skidded in the water-sodden street. He received concussion and an injured shoulder, but failed to report sick for two days.

In Southwark most of the fires that broke out were in residential areas, particularly in the area which runs south from the Elephant and Castle parallel with the New Kent Road.

The following day, 21 September, was a quieter day for London with heavier raids at night. However, six people were killed at the Wardens' Post at St Mary's church, Peckham, including wardens Henry Courtney, Handley Stevens and Samuel Bradley along with ambulance driver Harry Watts. Several persons were killed at Llewellyn Street at Dockhead while there were no casualties in Southwark.

The Charlsley family lived at No. 355 Lordship Lane, East Dulwich. The ground floor was the workshop and sales room of George Charlsley, who had a small watchmaking business. The family home was on the two floors above.

On 24 September the family were in the workshop when their cat's ears pricked up and it made a dart for the cellar. Quickly realising the cat's sixth sense, the family were hot on the cat's heels – in good time too as a landmine exploded in Woodwarde Road. The post office was wrecked, as were the two-storey public toilets by Dulwich Library. Neighbouring Etherow Street was a complete mess. Several people were killed in the incident as possibly might have been the Charlsley family, had it not been for the family pet.[x]

Bombing was reported as light in London on 28 September, but up at Denmark Hill School, now an AFS station, sixteen of the auxiliaries were taking no chances and were ensconced in the air-raid shelter. In the watchroom were auxiliaries Kathleen Smith and Grace Jessup. Suddenly there was an almighty explosion; the shelter had been hit by a high-explosive bomb. The watchroom was only a few feet from the shelter. Despite the watchroom being sandbagged, all the windows were blown out, the blackout curtains were down and the two women were covered in plaster.

Smith immediately got on the phone to report the direct hit then helped Jessup restore the blackout curtains.

The injuries to their colleagues were severe. Smith had recently taken a first-aid course, and this was the first chance to put her new skills to the test. Despite all her efforts, for which she was highly praised, thirteen of her colleagues were killed in the shelter.

In Great Guildford Street stood a little chapel; in its crypt was Wardens' Post 5. On 29 September, all was fine and the wardens were in fine fettle having attended a wedding during in the day. Albert Clark had signed on for his first shift a few hours earlier. It was to be his only shift. The chapel was struck by a high-explosive bomb, killing nine of the ten wardens on duty, Sydney Taylor being the only survivor, who was blown out of the entrance passage by the blast.

Among those killed were the popular Cheeseman brothers, Albert and Thomas; their father, Henry, was also killed. Another pair of brothers perished – Fred and Tom Darvell.

The chapel and Wardens' Post was demolished, taking rescue squads many hours, working in relays, to dig out the bodies. A small street not far away was renamed 'Wardens' Grove'. Sadly, it is a rather grubby dead-end street and not really a fitting memorial to those who were killed in the post. However, the Cheeseman brothers do have a memorial in the old Southwark Town Hall in Walworth Road.

The first month of the 'Night Blitz' was over. London and Londoners had certainly suffered. From 6 September to 30 September 1940, the total number of persons killed in the three boroughs was 620.

The opening days of October 1940 were not without incident in the three boroughs, but there was not the intensity or ferocity of the opening first weeks of the Night Blitz.

A heavy raid was delivered across London on 8 October. Bermondsey suffered with fires at Bellamy's Wharf, Jennings' Wharf and Wilson's Wharf, the latter being gutted. However, there were no deaths at these incidents.

With the Luftwaffe active along the riverfront Southwark also received its fair share of attention; the Peacock public house in Hopton Street, near the Bankside Power Station, took a direct hit. Air Raid Warden John Stacey was killed in this incident, as was Warden Jane Kirwan, the first female warden to be killed in Southwark. The blast hit Jane so hard that it blew her feet off. She was rushed to Guy's Hospital where she died of her wounds.

Shelter life was becoming a ritual with queues forming from mid-afternoon. Hannah Taylor of Peckham had written poetry all her life, none of which had been published. In the shelter at the Blenheim Grove railway arch she would read some of these to her new-found friends. She would produce an old exercise book and keep her audience spellbound with her writing, almost impervious to the noise and devastation going on outside. She wrote the following in 1916, the year of the Battle of the Somme:

Forward! Onward! Upward!
And though your hearts may break
Faith can pierce the densest mist that hides the highest peak
And you cross death' silver streak
Earth will be just a little better
For your climb towards the peak.[xi]

A very sobering poem to the listener and shelter-dweller in the dark days of 1940.

11 October was a tough night for the Southwark Civil Defence Services. At 8.15 a.m. Sumner Street Buildings was hit with by a high-explosive bomb. Fire from the gas main had broken out in front of one of the tenement blocks where 200 persons were sheltering. Attempts to effect any release of the shelterers would rely on the supply being turned off, which eventually happend. There was a report of persons trapped in another part of the building and a rescue party was working on this. Despite initially fearing the worst, the death toll was only eight persons in an incident that could have been much worse.

Nutt Street was a small street leading off Sumner Road, Peckham, again within a few minutes' walk from the Old Kent Road Gas Works. A high-explosive bomb hit the junction with Sumner Road and Shields Street. Four persons were killed at Nos 29 and 31.

The following night in Bermondsey, Young's Glue Works in Grange Road, which had already had some near squeaks including an unexploded bomb in the September, suffered the death of six of the workforce who were killed in an incident.

The Millpond Estate in Jamaica Road was badly damaged on 14 October with five persons killed in Millstream House. The block was rebuilt after the war with a curious reminder of the Blitz. The story is unknown, but a gargoyle from the destroyed House of Commons now appears on top of the rebuilt block.

Dennis Gardner, former Peckham resident, was a delivery boy for a newsagent in Caulfield Road. He recalls,

On the morning of 15 October the siren sounded and I finished my deliveries in the street I was in and started to make my way back to the shop.

On the way I could see German aircraft in the sky and bombs leaving the planes. I carried on cycling into Caulfield Road, because the shop was at the bottom of the street where it met Lugard Road.

The next thing I can remember was being taken to St Giles' Hospital, Camberwell. A bomb had hit a house as I was cycling past. I had cuts on the forehead and back of the head. Also my wrist was cut and my arm was injured. They told me afterwards that my greatest concern was whether my bike was ok? I was an out-patient at St Giles' until 19 November.

It was more tragic at the hospital that morning, for a food factory in Camberwell had been hit and lots of young girls, the workers, had lost their lives or were severely cut.[xii]

Dennis was referring to the direct hit on H. S. Whiteside and Co. Ltd, manufacturing confectioners, who also produced the famous Sun-Pat peanut butter. Six of the workforce were killed, including fifteen-year-old Elsie Crawley and seventeen-year-old Violet Parsons. Many, as Dennis Gardner remembered, were injured.

Florence Parker lost the use of her left arm as a result of the incident at Whiteside's. Her comment to the *South London Press* was 'What's the use of moping about it?'

Sixteen-year-old Jean Hughes was severely burnt at Whiteside's by a stream of scalding glucose. She was so close to death that a member of the clergy was summoned to her hospital bedside. She survived forty-eight hours in a coma and underwent a series of skin grafts at the Queen Victoria Hospital, East Grinstead – the hospital was pioneered by Archibald McIndoe for RAF personnel who had been badly burnt in action and needed this revolutionary surgery.

15 October 1940 was a horrendous day for neighbouring Lambeth; the Kennington Park trench shelters took a direct hit, as did the Morley College Rest Centre. Upwards of 150 persons were killed in the two incidents.

Queen's Buildings in Scovell Road and Collinson Street at the borough were primarily social housing. Tall tenement buildings dominated the streets – homes to working-class folk, many of whom would have been working in the local brewing and hop trade.

At 1.14 a.m. on 16 October a parachute mine silently descended onto Queen's Buildings, Scovell Road, and exploded. The result was horrific. Initial reports told of two shelters hit, and an estimate of 100 people trapped and 50 other casualties.

Local beat policeman PC William Keery was swift into action; when he arrived at the scene he was told of cries from a cellar. A small opening was discovered and debris and iron railings were removed and the opening was enlarged, allowing Keery to drop down into the cellar. The scene which greeted him was a tangled mess of fallen beams and masonry. Keery picked his way through to reach the trapped victims. With great danger to himself he was able to bring out alive a badly injured man, three children and a woman, and lastly went back for two more men – all this while bombs were still being dropped in the area.

Making light of his efforts in the cellar, which must have exhausted him; he worked through the night helping the Civil Defence Service personnel in their work.

Henry Varley's family lived at the Oval. His father had a print shop in a basement in Scovell Road. The father, an auxiliary fireman on the embankment, had a feeling that a big raid would occur that night and sent his family to shelter at the print shop. Mr Varley was correct in his assumption but hadn't banked on the parachute mine floating silently down to where he had sent his family. Henry, aged five at the time, can remember being brought out of the rubble on a fireman's shoulders. His younger sister, Yvonne, was also rescued but was taken to Guy's Hospital with perforated eardrums. It was a lucky escape for the Varley youngsters.

Forty-two persons lost their lives at Queen's Buildings with many more injured. The damage to property was extensive. Scovell Road is now a modern estate with no reminder of the horror that occurred over seventy years ago.

St John's church stands back off Goose Green in East Dulwich Road. The church was gutted on 19 October. The vicar in the war years was Frank Bishop. He wrote, 'On October 19th, 1940, a load of incendiaries were dropped over Goose Green and four separate fires were started on the church roof. With the help of men from the National Fire Service stationed at Adys Road School, we managed to get them all out and soon had the roof repaired and church clean.'[xiii]

Little did Frank know that the Luftwaffe had more in store for this fine church.

Bermondsey Council were proud of the title they were given pre-war: 'The London Borough of Shelter.' Their boast was that they could provide shelter, in the event of war, for 55,000 of its population, including the use of railway arches, which spanned down from London Bridge through Deptford, New Cross and beyond. This boast was to bite them on the foot on more than one occasion, not just as with the Linsey Street Arch incident earlier in the Night Blitz.

Druid Street Arch housed a billiard hall. By night it was a rest centre for those bombed out and was also a shelter. At 9 p.m. on 25 October a high-explosive bomb pierced the railway and exploded. The explosion also ignited a gas main in the road by the entrance to the arch. A furious fire prevented rescue squads from carrying out their much-needed work. By the time the gas main was turned off, the bomb had done its deadly job as eighty-seven were killed, gas and fire creating a deadly cocktail for those trapped. This was to be Bermondsey's worst single incident in terms of persons killed during the war. Six children under one year of age were among those killed; two of the children were four months old, these being John Brown and Derrick Johnson. Entire families were killed in this most tragic of incidents. A plaque amid the lock-ups and repair shops in Druid Street is a sad reminder to a lesson that wasn't learnt.

Standing on the north junction of Union Street and Blackfriars Road was 'The Ring' boxing and wrestling arena. It was formerly the Surrey chapel and its founder was the eccentric preacher Rowland Hill. The chapel was of a circular design 'so the Devil couldn't hide in the corner'.

The chapel closed in 1881, but became a famous sporting arena in 1910.

On 25 October, a high-explosive bomb penetrated the railway line that runs from London Bridge to Waterloo East. Six trams were sheltering under the bridge; three were demolished and the remainder badly damaged. Several people were also killed. The Ring was also a casualty; badly damaged, it had to be demolished. In pre-war days, the pub on the opposite corner was named 'The Railway'. The name was changed to 'The Ring' after the war and the first floor became a boxing gymnasium. Negley Farson, an American writer, commented on one of his tours of blitzed London that the pub served some of the finest sausages in London.

St Peter's church is situated in Liverpool Grove, just off Walworth Road. The local community were tight-knit, many living on the Church Commissioners' Estate, which was built in the early 1900s. Many of the original tenants' children had grown up, gotten married and raised their own families on the same estate. St Peter's was the hub of the community, and the vicar was John Markham, a popular man and friend to all; he was also in charge of the local Air Raid Wardens' Post.

The Luftwaffe was still active over Bermondsey, Camberwell and Southwark towards the end of October, but Southwark bore the brunt of the raid of 29 October. The courtyards of the estate had their own shelters but were not numerous enough or large enough to accommodate all. Therefore, St Peter's large crypt was an obvious choice for the overspill and other locals.

There were reported to have been 400 persons in the shelter on the night of 28/29 October. At 1.40 p.m. on the 29th, three high-explosive bombs smashed through the roof, through the church floor and exploded in the crypt. The scene was one of mayhem. The death toll was officially recorded as sixty-seven, with 250 injured. As with many incidents that had gone before, entire families perished and the whole local community felt the loss of friends and neighbours personally. The death toll could have been higher. The arches in the crypt supporting the body of the church were of a circular design; these almost acted as suspension springs that prevented a wholesale collapse of the church.

As the rescue services were pulling the dead out of the crypt and laying them in the churchyard, John Markham was a sickened man as many of these were his friends as well as parishioners.

November 1940 brought a change in tactics by the Luftwaffe; London was still bombed but much of the attention changed to the industrial Midlands.

November brought nine deaths in Bermondsey, fifteen in Camberwell and ten in Southwark. This was a far cry from the combined total of September to October, which was 1,078. November also brought to an end to fifty-seven consecutive nights of bombing for Londoners.

With a harsh winter set to follow, the Luftwaffe was literally back with a bang on 8/9 December 1940, particularly in Bermondsey. Extensive damage occurred on the 8th at Scott's Sufferance Wharf, the Grange, houses and factories in Riley Road, Mark Brown's Warehouse in Potter's Fields, St George's Hall and Lloyd's in Bermondsey Street to name but a few. The shelter at the John Bull Arch at 'The Blue' took a direct hit with sixteen persons killed.

Revd Frank Bishop picks up the story of his church, St John's, Goose Green, East Dulwich Road:

On Sunday, December 8th, another load of larger variety, some of which were explosive, descended. We were inside within one minute of their coming down. But only one had come through the roof. Many must have remained in it, for almost at once, it was alight from end to end. There were fires everywhere that night and it was three quarters of an hour before the first appliance arrived and about another four or five hours before the firemen had got the fire out.[xiv]

The church was badly gutted and restored after the war. There is the customary First World War memorial inside the church to a number of local men killed in that conflict. Underneath is a further memorial to local men killed serving in the Second

World War. A further touching tribute to these men are six candleholders on the altar dedicated to their memory.

A happy event was being planned at No. 37 Nunhead Lane on 9 December. Wedding plans were being discussed for the double wedding at Christmas for the daughters of Mr and Mrs Flockton, Ellen and Beatrice, to their intended bridegrooms, Eric Smith and Pte Alfred Stocking.

The evening of planning was shattered by a high-explosive bomb landing in Nunhead Lane, and all thoughts turned to the girls' aunt, Ellen Fautley, who was killed in the blast. Her husband, Henry, was badly injured in the incident, and several family members were treated for minor injuries.

The story had a happy ending: though the double weddings didn't take place as planned at Christmas, but both went ahead in 1941.[xv]

The receiving hospital for Camberwell, St Giles', was having problems of its own on 8 December. At 11.16 p.m. the hospital was rocked by a high-explosive bomb; the entire hospital fell into darkness, A Block was demolished and debris was everywhere with many members of staff trapped. The rescue service, however, prevailed, and all those trapped were released, and the receiving ward, lit with hurricane lamps, was quickly made ready to treat the injured.

Probationer nurse Elizabeth Scully was in A1 Ward when the bomb struck. The entrance to the ward was blocked with debris, and the only available option was to escape through a window. Nurse Scully was wounded in the leg and foot, but despite her injuries she was able to assess the situation and get three elderly and frail patients through the window to safety.

Elizabeth Scully went on to have quite a career after the war. In 1946 she entered the convent and started to run St Joseph's Industrial School in Ballinasloe, Galway, in 1951. Money was always short, and she was often seen doing repairs, much to the hilarity of colleagues and the children. When the school closed in 1967 she continued to work in the infirmary until 1970, when she took over the local 'meals on wheels' service. Despite losing a leg through illness, she continued delivering the service, driving over 100 miles each day. This work continued until she turned eighty-two. She was awarded the 'Heart of Gold' award, one of many in her long and distinguished life. This marvellous person, affectionately known as the 'Old Trout', died on 1 May 2009, at age ninety-two. The *Irish Independent* described the funeral as 'A grand occasion, but it was also spiritual and heartbreakingly sad.'[xvi]

Leonard Rogers was the popular manager of a hostel in Sylvester Street, Southwark, working there with his father. On 9 December a small high-explosive bomb lodged itself on top of the building. Leonard went up to the top of the building to remove it. As he grasped it, the bomb exploded, killing him instantly. The father of two was a bitter loss to his family and residents of the hostel. Tenant W. A. MacSweeney paid tribute to Leonard Rogers, saying, 'He gave his whole for us. No man could do more. His act was to save the poor fellows of the hostel.'[xvii]

The raid of 8/9 December 1940 was the last big raid in the run-up to Christmas. With the ever-deteriorating weather on the Continent, it was becoming more and more difficult for the Luftwaffe to get their raids away from their grass airfields.

A nervy Christmas Day and Boxing Day came and passed, but 27 December brought the Luftwaffe knocking on London's door again. Grace Smith Grogan recalls,

It was the day following Boxing Day 1940. I was 21 years old and living in my parents' house, 9 Fenwick Road. We were enjoying our evening meal when strange sounds like fireworks swishing down to the ground excited us.

Some of us rushed into the garden; others to the front of the house.

These were incendiary bombs blazing a trail to light up the black-out for the bombers following along behind. The whole street was filled with people frantically putting the fires out. We then noticed a fire bomb on our roof. My father rushed up five flights of stairs to the top back bedroom. He jumped through the sky-light, put the bomb in a pail of earth and carried it spluttering into the garden and buried it.

We stood warming in front of a coal fire when suddenly all hell opened up. Bombs came raining down. Suddenly there was a terrific noise. 'This is it,' called my father, 'This is ours!' The house trembled and a wall fell down away from us. We scrambled out to the front door to be met by just a gap. We stood in the front garden and looked straight through to the back garden. We thanked God that we were still alive.

We faced the back of the King's Arms public house. A land mine had fallen and the parachute had tangled in a tree; it then exploded. The whole area was practically demolished as were the very large houses in East Dulwich Road.[xviii]

Bus conductors Harold Wizgell and Richard Sibley were enjoying a break at the end of their routes in a café at No. 6 East Dulwich Road when the landmine struck and caused the premises to collapse. The café was owned by a Mr Umney, whose wife and children were in a shelter at the rear.

With debris falling, Wizgell and Sibley rushed to the shelter and pulled out Mr Umney's family. There were rumours that a man and woman, Arthur and Florence Masters, were trapped in an adjoining property. The only entrance (because of the fallen debris) was though a window that had a grill covering it. Somehow Wizgell managed to prise the bars open enough to crawl through and Sibley followed him in, and with the help of PC George Whitmore, War Reserve PC Ernest Gilbert and Air Raid Warden Henry Hicks, three-quarters of an hour later they managed to dig out Mr Masters. Wizgell emerged choking and exhausted, and his work in trying to locate Mrs Masters was taken up by Whitmore, Ernest Gilbert and Hicks.

The three worked tirelessly, passing rubble and debris back through the tunnel they had created. Finally, Mrs Masters was located, but she was pinned down by a large slab of marble and an iron bar. With great effort, and much difficulty, Mrs Masters was finally freed and passed back to other police officers at the other end of the tunnel. She was rushed to hospital where she pronounced dead.

The landmine completely demolished Nos 6–10 East Dulwich Road, damaging many other properties. The area has been completely rebuilt after the war, with modern properties on the junction of East Dulwich Road and Fenwick Road. Ten persons were killed in Camberwell in this raid, primarily in the East Dulwich area.

Bermondsey was bombed on this night, but was primarily subjected to incendiary bombs with little serious damage reported.

In Southwark, a small area around East Street was hit by a considerable amount of incendiary bombs and several high-explosive bombs. Amazingly, there was only one death – in nearby Inville Road. Seventeen-year-old Eileen Mulligan worked as a telephonist at Southwark Control in Walworth Road; she doubled up as a volunteer warden in her spare time. With the telephone lines down, Eileen worked as bicycle messenger between the Wardens' Post in Wooler Street and the control centre. Bombs were still falling while she was cycling through the back streets of Walworth.

Her deed having been done, she helped the rescue services at a bombed shelter in Burton Grove; being petite enough to squeeze through a gap, she rendered first aid to some of the trapped.

Two days prior, Adolf Hitler had Christmas lunch with his senior staff in Boulogne. Questions were raised as to why Britain was not looking to come to the peace table? Why the spirit of the British people had not been broken? The result was the ordering of a large post-Christmas attack on London on 29 December.

It was a weekend over the Christmas period. Not many properties were adequately watched. With Southwark and Bermondsey located just south of the City of London, it was inevitable that these two boroughs were also going to experience a tough night. One Southwark Air Raid Warden remarked, 'Everything that missed the City seemed to hit Southwark!'

In Southwark, the Blackfriars Road end of Southwark Street was particularly badly hit with a huge loss of property in the vicinity as incendiary bombs took their toll on the old warehouses that adorned the long stretch of road along to Blackfriars Goods Yard.

From one of the warehouses a man was seen staggering out of a blaze and collapsing. Among those fighting the conflagration were Sub-Officer John Cornford and Station Officer Arthur Thorne. On seeing the beleaguered man, they sprinted a good distance through flames and falling debris to bring him to safety. One slip from either of them could have resulted in their own demise. The unknown casualty died as a result of his injuries. This was possibly Richard Cowan who died at No. 75 Southwark Street, although reports suggest that the man died in King's College Hospital, though there is nothing official to support this.

Running north to south, Keyworth Street lies behind the Elephant and Castle station. Much of the area is now dominated by the modern buildings of the South Bank University. The street was originally named Danzig Street, but was rechristened Keyworth Street in memory of First World War Victoria Cross winner Leonard Keyworth, who served with the local 24th Battalion of the London Regiment. Lennie won his Victoria Cross at Givenchy on 25/26 May 1915 only to die from wounds at the Battle of Loos later that year. Lennie also has local Keyworth Street School named after him.

At 7.35 p.m. the air-raid shelter in Keyworth Street took a direct hit with twelve persons losing their lives. Many were trapped and rescue squads worked manfully into the night to free these persons.

On the border of Southwark and Bermondsey, Women's Auxiliary Fire Service's Margaret Miller and Margaret Hamer were on duty at their station in Searles Road near the Bricklayer's Arms. As a high-explosive bomb exploded on Tilling's Garage, both were blown on to the floor, covered with dust, plaster and glass, and the lighting failed. Hamer immediately lit hurricane lamps. Residents of Searles Road burst into the station – as often civilians rushed to places of authority – many injured with cuts. Hamer had recently completed a first-aid course and immediately began calming down the locals and tending to their wounds. While the injured were being looked after, Miller coolly maintained communications with control as the direct line was undamaged, ordered what was required and set about helping Hamer with the first-aid treatment.

Fires were also raging around the borough. Westbury's Cane works was located at No. 199a Borough High Street. The cane in the company stores was for use in the fireworks industry. At 8.24 p.m. Westbury's was hit by an incendiary bomb; the highly flammable cane accentuated the blaze, and it was three days before the Fire Service could get near the blaze. The result was devastating: a company memo suggests, 'The entire stock and offices at 199 Borough High Street were destroyed by enemy action on the night of 29/30 December 1940.'[xix]

The company relocated temporarily to New Cross and Clapham.

Parts of Camberwell were not exempt from the devastation taking place in the City and riverside boroughs just across the Thames. De Crespigny Park is opposite King's College Hospital in Demark Hill. No. 26 took a direct hit from a high-explosive bomb, killing Luigi Del Nevo and his five-year-old daughter Maureen, along with auxiliary fireman Martin Wright, his wife Amelia and their two-year-old son Martin Jnr.

Next door, No. 24, was partially destroyed with the roof blown off. Three police officers were sent to investigate from Camberwell Police Station – Sergeants Dorrington and Daddy along with PC Charles Mann.

On arrival they found one of the occupants, Mr Sterckx, leaning out of an upstairs window, yelling for help. The houses in De Crespigny Park have several storeys and are tall, grand buildings. Consequently, the window Sterckx was 30 feet from the ground – too far to jump safely. All other possible exits were blocked by debris. Mann found a ladder, which he placed against the wall, but this was still around 12 feet short of the window where Sterckx was. Mann scaled the ladder and stretched from the top rung, but was still too far away to bring Sterckx to safety. Mann managed to lever himself a little higher by placing one foot on a shattered ground-floor window frame. He was now close enough to encourage the trapped man to climb out of the window and lower a leg onto his right hand. He carefully guided Sterckx onto the ladder, and both were able to climb down from this precarious position.

Charles Mann was awarded the George Medal for his bravery. It also has to be remembered that bombs were still falling in the area during the rescue. Making light of his bravery, Mann told the *South London Press* that he hoped the award would help in his application to train as a pilot in the Fleet Air Arm.

Charles Mann did leave the Police, not to join Fleet Air Arm but 32 Elementary Flying Training School based in Bowden, Alberta. The Squadron Diary has a sad entry dated 4 August 1942: 'LAC Mann, CGT T/T Pilot (51 course) overturned a service transport in Penhold Village and injuring six airman he had picked up.' Charles George Toni Mann is buried in Innisfail Cemetery, Alberta.

Loncroft Road was situated among a maze of streets just south of Albany Road. The area was home to terraced housing and light and medium industry. Also, the old Surrey Canal ran east–west through the area parallel with St George's Way. As a stick of high explosives fell across the area, fourteen persons were killed in the street and the shelter. There were also casualties in nearby streets such as Southampton Way.

High-explosive bombs landed outside Camberwell Town Hall in Peckham Road, killing a number of people including Air Raid Wardens Charles Darlington, Ernest Follett, William Newcombe and John Owens. Also among the casualties were a group of Polish service personnel whose coach had stopped because of the raid. The Conservative club in Vestry Mews across the road was destroyed by an oil bomb.

In Bermondsey, a high-explosive bomb demolished part of a block of Devon Mansions, a well-known social housing estate, killing residents at Nos 277 and 299. A plaque on the wall where the incident occurred is a reminder of 29 December 1940.

Although the attack was delivered on the City of London, it was a tough night for Camberwell and Southwark with forty-five deaths in the former and seventeen in the latter.

There were supposed to be two raids on 29 December 1940, but with the bad weather and the poor state of the runways on the German airfields across the Channel, a second raid was not possible. If the second raid had materialised, the consequences would have been unthinkable if it had been delivered with the aplomb of the first.

With the stumps drawn on 1940, Bermondsey, Camberwell and Southwark had certainly seen a huge amount of destruction to their homes and their industries. The civilian death toll in the first four months of the Night Blitz was as follows:

Bermondsey   376
Camberwell   449
Southwark   434

A total of 1,259 persons killed for the three boroughs.

A comparison with neighbouring boroughs for the same period can be seen below:

Deptford   213
Lambeth   739
Lewisham   399

Bermondsey Civil Defence Personnel. Joe Blake is third from the left in the front row. (Southwark Local Studies Library)

Above: Keetons Road was also hit in the air raids of the First World War. (Southwark Local Studies Library)

Opposite above: Fort Road, Bermondsey in 1946. (Southwark Local Studies Library)

Opposite below: Keetons Road School after the high-explosive bombs struck on 8 September 1940. (Southwark Local Studies Library)

Damage to Llewellyn Street, September 1940. (Southwark Local Studies Library)

Modern-day Llewellyn Street. (Author's collection)

Clearing up the damage in Neptune Street, September 1940. (Southwark Local Studies Library)

Air-raid shelter converted to garages on the Dhonau Estate, Dunton Road. (Author's Collection)

Firefighters attempting to tackle a blazing warehouse on 7 September 1940. (Southwark Local Studies Library)

Blue plaque to the Druid Street Arch bombing, 25 October 1940. (Author's collection)

Grave of John Ivison in Camberwell New Cemetery, killed in the landmine incident at the West Bermondsey Labour Institute on 18 September 1940. (Author's collection)

Above: An Emergency Water Supply sign on the former John Wilson's Grammar School in Camberwell. (Author's collection)

Opposite above: A dramatic cloud of smoke over Peckham. (Southwark Local Studies Library)

Opposite below: 'Wings for Victory Week' display in Rye Lane, 1940. (Southwark Local Studies Library)

The destroyed St Mary's church, Nunhead, where six members of the Wardens' Service were killed on 21 September 1940. (Southwark Local Studies Library)

Modern-day St Mary's church, Nunhead. (Author's collection)

In memory of the people of Camberwell who died or suffered in War

This memorial stands above the Air Raid Shelter where a wedding party lost their lives on the afternoon of 17 September 1940.

Sidney and Patricia Wright had just married and were celebrating in the nearby 'Father Redcap' Public House with family and friends.

During an air raid, they sought refuge in the shelter which was directly hit by a bomb. All members of the Wright family and four other people were killed.

May they and all victims of War, rest in peace

Memorial to the wedding party killed in the shelter on Camberwell Green. (Southwark Local Studies Library)

The gutted Queen's Buildings, Scovell Road, after the landmine of 16 October 1940. (Southwark Local Studies Library)

The Scovell Road Estate today, unrecognisable from pre-war years. (Author's collection)

The destroyed Metropolitan Public House on the junction of Southwark Street and Southwark Bridge Road. (Southwark Local Studies Library)

The modern Southwark Rooms on the same junction. (Author's collection)

Above: 'The Ring' in Blackfriars Road, destroyed on 25 October 1940. (Southwark Local Studies Library)

Opposite: The modern replacement for The Ring – the Palestra Building, home of Transport for London. (Author's collection)

The West Bermondsey Labour Institute before its destruction on 18 September 1940. (Southwark Local Studies Library)

Shrapnel damage on the railway bridge across Blackfriars Road. (Author's collection)

No. 89 Southwark Street was gutted on 29 December 1940. (Southwark Local Studies Library)

The modern replacement at No. 89 Southwark Street. (Author's collection)

Memorial scroll to those killed in the crypt at St Peter's Church, Merrow Street, on 20 October 1940. (Author's collection)

A burnt-out Westbury's Cane Co., destroyed on 29 December 1940. (Southwark Local Studies Library)

The John Harvard Library now stands on the site of Westbury's. (Author's collection)

1941
A Deadly Spring

The winter of 1940/41 was a severe one. The New Year celebrations, though probably somewhat muted, had passed. A quieter time than the fury of 27 and 29 December was enjoyed by the residents of Camberwell as the Air Raid Wardens' log recorded 'nil' incidents until 7 January.

However, the Luftwaffe paid a visit to Bermondsey on 5 January. A wake-up call in the shape of two high-explosive bombs hit the Grange and caused considerable damage to a range of houses, some of which had been earmarked for demolition because of previous raids. Three people sheltering in the condemned properties were killed: William Bissett, Walter Newman and fifteen-year-old Reggie Swann. Reggie was the son of Rose and the late Baylis Swann, the latter had been killed at the Royal Oak, Maltby Street, on 9 September 1940. The Grange Mission Hall, being used a first aid post, was also damaged; thankfully for the local population, most of the first aid equipment survived the blasts. The Grange has been totally rebuilt as has much of this part of Bermondsey, and long gone is the evidence of the tanning and leather industry that dominated the pre-war area.

With the weather slightly improving, the Luftwaffe were back over the skies of London from 9 January. Hartley's Jam Factory, in Green Walk off Tower Bridge Road, had been relatively unscathed in 1940. Tonight was the famous factory's turn to feel the might of the Luftwaffe. At 7.20 p.m. a high-explosive burst between the factory's shelter and B block of the factory. Four employees were killed, ironically non-residents of the borough. Many other workers were buried and rescued from the wreckage, with over fifty people hurt or requiring first aid. Fireman George Grove also died two days later of injuries sustained at the incident.

The Luftwaffe were still coming, but without the regularity and perhaps without the ferocity of September and October 1940.

11 January brought a bigger raid, particularly across parts of Southwark and Bermondsey, with a cocktail of incendiary bombs and high explosives. The dockland

area was yet again in the firing line, with incendiary bombs hitting Albin's Undertakers, Mark Brown's Warehouse, Williams' Engineers, Carlutt's Wharf among many other industrial and residential buildings. Thirty incendiary bombs were reported around London Bridge Station. Casualties were light, although two people were killed at Meggeson's Factory in Llewellyn Street as two high-explosive bombs found their mark.

The Luftwaffe was on the mark in Southwark also, particularly in the north-west part of the borough on the border with Lambeth. In Lambeth Road, a high-explosive bomb hit the Lady of Consolation Hospital; adjoining properties were also damaged, and a tram was totally destroyed in the blast. Four of the hospital nursing staff lost their lives, including sixty-five-year-old Sister Catherina Babe.

A quiet run through to the end of January 1941 was had by all in the three boroughs. There were raids, and casualties included local council employee Lancelot Smith and his friend, Ada Casemore, who lost their lives in Sturgeon Road, Southwark, on 16 January. The luckiest person in the property was a Mr C. Smith, who only received a black eye from the blast.

The Druid Street Arch incident of October 1940 was to come back and haunt Bermondsey in February 1941. Raiding had been very light in the early days of the month. Stainer Street railway arch runs under London Bridge Station from St Thomas Street to Tooley Street, a distance of a couple of hundred yards. The plans to utilise the arch as a large shelter went back to the pre-war days of the late thirties. It could house several hundred people. By this time, shelters of this size required adequate toilet facilities and a medical post staffed by qualified personnel. Dr Lesley Probyn from Pontypool, south wales, who had qualified as a doctor in 1926. One of her roles was to inspect shelters with medical facilities and insure conditions were up to standard. She was held in high regard by her colleagues and seniors. She was making an inspection on the evening of 17 February 1941.

Jimmy Chandler also visited Stainer Street shelter on this night. Jimmy, aged fifteen, was a popular young man who doted on his father and grandmother. A speedway fan, Jimmy rarely went out but arranged to meet some friends to play darts in the recreation area set aside in the shelter.[i]

Part of the blast protection for the shelter were 5-ton steel doors at each end of the arch, which were deemed adequate protection from any high-explosive bombs landing in the streets around the arch.

At 10.25 p.m. a high-explosive bomb pierced the railway above the arch at the St Thomas Street end and exploded within. With the steel doors being pulled inwards with the blast, all hell broke loose; the doors tore along the arch, acting almost as a meat grinder to all in their path. Some 300 people were reputed to be sheltering in the arch, sixty-eight of whom were killed and a further 175 injured. The bodies of Lesley Probyn and her two Red Cross nursing colleagues, Rosina Hartley and

Ethel Little, were never found. Home-loving Jimmy Chandler lost his life along with a number of teenagers, who were more than likely his friends.

Those sixty-eight killed, whether their bodies were recovered on not, were known to be in the shelter or could be identified. It is probable that more were killed than the number given, with passers-by ducking into the shelter at the height of the raid. The arch is in the shadow of Guy's Hospital, whose doctors and nurses worked manfully alongside the rescue services, tending to the wounded as they were brought out. Ironically, Guy's was the receiving hospital for Southwark, but the arch was just across the border in Bermondsey.

To compound the incident, a delayed-action bomb exploded just after 4 a.m. the following morning near the White Hart public house on the corner of St Thomas Street and Great Maze Pond. Two young members of the Wardens' Service, Charles Heron and John Shepherd, were killed.

Sixteen-year-old Elsie Payne, known to all as 'Chick', loved life and loved dancing. She was the popular Girl Guides Patrol Leader of St James's church in Jamaica Road. On 8 March 1941, Elsie and her friends, Eileen Graham and Lily Kendall, had been to a dance at the Clubland church in Camberwell during the late afternoon. There was a dance later that the girls were invited to and wanted to attend. Elsie and Lily lived in Fort Buildings, Southwark Park Road, and Eileen in West Dulwich. They needed permission to stay out for the later dance. A young Wardens' Post stretcher-bearer escorted the girls most of the way home.

The date was 8 March 1941; that night the Luftwaffe decided to break their almost three-week gap in visits to Bermondsey. As the excited girls reached the entrance to Fort Buildings, a high-explosive bomb destroyed the block, killing all three. The death toll at the incident was eighteen. Others killed included Lily's younger sister, Ivy, and two young fire-watchers, Henry Hughes and Ernest Fricker, at their post in the arched entrance to the block.

Speaking to the *South London Press*, Elsie Payne's grief-stricken mother said, 'She had no fear and always said, "Well, if a bomb gets me it's the finish."' Sadly, this tragic incident was 'the finish' for a girl with a bright future and all to live for. There is no reminder of the incident at the scene. What was Fort Buildings is now part of the Harris Academy's playing fields.[ii]

Manor Place, just of the Walworth Road, housed the depot for the Southwark Rescue Services along with a civil defence canteen, particularly enjoyed by the wardens from Post 12 in Amelia Street.

At 8.25 p.m. on 8 March, a high-explosive bomb hit Nos 156–162 Manor Place; these three-storey houses were poor quality and just crumbled away from the blast. Many were trapped, and rescue services worked manfully to free them. A woman protested that the wardens were not doing enough to assist the rescue service, but was politely told that this kind of work should left to those who knew their business.

There was no hope for those who were in the houses that were hit directly by the blast. Seven people were killed in Nos 160 and 162.

The middle of March 1941 was a busier period for Camberwell than the earlier days of the month. In not a heavy raid by 1940 standards, the Luftwaffe paid a visit on the 15th, particularly to Peckham.

Kirkwood Road runs up to Nunhead from Queen's Road. At precisely 10 p.m., No. 145 took a direct hit from a high-explosive bomb, resulting in the rear of the premises being demolished. The police attended the incident and assumed that all rescue work was proceeding according to plan. About an hour later, it was discovered that a young girl, five-and-a-half-year-old Joan Barry, was still trapped under a mass of debris. Off set Sergeant Trott and PCs Leslie and Kerr from Peckham police station back to Kirkwood Road. On arrival, they found rescue party member Edward Scanlon frantically trying to tunnel down to Joan, but he was unable to do this on his own. PC James Leslie immediately entered the tunnel armed with a police jack with Scanlon behind him. Work was painfully slow as both men were on their stomachs and were only able to operate using one arm. As Leslie operated the jack, Scanlon pulled out the debris from the tunnel and both men propped up the tunnel with wooden struts.

Meanwhile, Trott and Kerr were trying to reach Joan from above. Leslie and Scanlon were still not in a position to reach Joan; contact was made by Leslie, and he comforted her by telling her stories. It was then discovered that Joan's arm was trapped by a piece of debris supporting a party wall; if disturbed, this may pull the wall down on top of all three of them. With a concerted effort in shifts, Joan was finally pulled out of the rubble an hour and a half later; she had a sore arm but otherwise was totally uninjured.

PC John Fleming was off duty in his home in Barkworth Road just behind the South-Eastern Gas Works. At around 9 p.m. on 18 March, a shower of around fifty incendiary bombs swooped down into the neighbouring area. Quickly, Fleming went up and extinguished two that had dropped on his own house. He rushed out of his house and began to help the attendant fire service put out others.

Several incendiaries had burst into life on the roof of No. 95 Barkworth Road, the home of ninety-year-old Mrs Tuck, who was bedridden with rheumatism. Local residents made unsuccessful attempts to fight their way into the property to free her – the smoke and heat being too much to bear.

Undeterred, Fleming charged into the house and ran up the stairs into a smoke-filled room. For what protection it offered, Fleming placed a handkerchief over his mouth and crawled around the room, looking for a bed. After being unsuccessful in his search of one room, he entered another, which was ablaze. He finally found Mrs Tuck and managed to pull her across the burning room, down the stairs and to safety, from where she was rushed to a nearby first aid post.

Raiding towards the end of March and into early April was light, but if the citizens of London thought they were going to have an easier time in spring months of 1941, they were to get a rude awakening.

A tough few nights were in store for the citizens of London. On the night of 16/17 April 1941, the Germans delivered the largest raid yet on the citizens of London. Nine hundred bombers operated over the skies of London that night; the damage caused and the number killed were fearful. Over 1,000 Londoners lost their lives.

Bermondsey fared better than Southwark or Camberwell, with casualties light in comparison. The Wardens' log for the borough shows a good number of incendiary bombs falling, which were dealt with quickly, and the damage recorded was slight in most cases. However, there were two serious incidents. The Royal Oak public house stood in Morgans Lane, running up towards the river. This stretch of Tooley Street had already received a nasty stick of incendiary bombs on 29 December 1940.

At twenty past midnight on 17 April a landmine descended silently through the clouds before finding its mark on the Royal Oak. Eight people were killed in the pub and neighbouring properties, with a further seventeen injured. The Wardens' log recorded 'extensive damage over 150 yards'. The area was devastated and as repairs were almost impossible, this part of the borough is unrecognisable from 1941.

At the corner of the Old Kent Road and Pages Walk, just where Bermondsey meets Southwark, there stood Arpino's Fruiters, a family-run business. A high-explosive bomb scored a direct hit in the row where the Fruiters was located. Proprietor Antonio Arpinio was killed alongside his twenty-year-old daughter Amelia, and thirteen-year-old son. Stephen Hall was killed in an adjoining property; there were four other people injured.

Southwark took a pounding this particular night; a cocktail of incendiary and high-explosive bombs brought death and destruction to the borough. The death toll was 101 people, approximately one-tenth of those killed London-wide.

Both sides of Walworth Road were badly hit. Crampton Street School was located a stone's throw from Wardens' Post 12 in Amelia Street. On 16 April, a high-explosive bomb exploded on the school, demolishing part of it. The school was used as a stretcher party depot. Post Warden Joshua Barham was first on the scene, and it was quickly realised that several of the walls were in danger of collapsing. Barham went into the dangerous part of the building, and working under one of the walls, he was able to free four members of the stretcher party. When help arrived, Barham was able to tell them where other members of the stretcher party were located. Despite Barham's and the rescue party's gallant efforts, twelve members of the depot were killed.

A slightly higher number were killed as two high-explosive bombs thundered into Grosvenor Terrace. Sixteen residents of this quiet terraced street lost their lives at Nos 71, 150 and 152. Entire families were killed. The incident was compounded by an unexploded bomb being located. This was later removed on 24 April.

Skipton Street formerly lay in the shadow of the Elephant and Castle underground station. The street is no longer there. Its cramped terraced housing has been replaced by modern offices and South Bank University premises.

At the end of 17 April 1941, more than twenty of the street's residents were dead. A high-explosive bomb scored a direct hit on a shelter and nearby houses. Many others were injured. Seven members of the Golder family were killed, including two-year-old John Crome, along with his parents, John and Phyllis. They all lived at Phyllis's parents' house, who were also killed. Five members of three generations of the Hassell family were also killed, including young Lilian, aged six. Floral tributes were laid by residents and friends for both the families. All told, twenty-nine people were killed, which includes other locals using the shelter. A modern office block, 'Skipton House', is a scant reminder to that night.[iii]

Blackfriars Road runs from St George's Circus up to Blackfriars Bridge. Set back on the western side is Christ church. Locals have been worshiping there for over 400 years. Blackfriars Road, on the night of 16/17 April, was subjected to a large stick of incendiary bombs. One of these lodged in the roof of the church; the resulting fire was devastating. First the roof caught fire, causing blazing roof timbers to fall into the heart of the church. Anything combustible caught fire. Church parishioners rushed to see what they could do to save their church. The heat so intense that the church bells melted. By the time the fire was out, all that was left was the shell of the church. Atop of the church was a wooden cross, which itself was on fire. It broke away from its mounting and landed bold upright in the churchyard; it stood there for some ten seconds before falling on to the grass. The *Daily Mirror*, at the time, described it as 'A fiery cross summoning the Highland clans to battle'.

When the blackened cross was moved, it left a charred cross-shaped imprint on the grass in the churchyard. Southwark Council had the char mark paved as a permanent memorial to the destroyed church. There is also a small plaque that relates some of the story.

The cut runs east to west from Blackfriars Road to Waterloo Road. It is right on the border of modern Southwark and Lambeth and has 'changed boroughs' over the course of the years. Walklin's Bakery was in a parade of shops about 150 yards from Southwark Station, now the site of the Young Vic Theatre.

The basement of the bakery was being used as a shelter during the Blitz; fifty-four people were settled in for the night. In one foul swoop, fifty-four people had lost their lives in the early hours of 17 April; a high-explosive bomb had dealt its deadly hand, with the bakery taking a direct hit.

Again, entire families were no more. A bomb does not respect age; casualties ranged from seventy-seven-year-old Emily Rumble down to two-month-old John Green. The incident was recorded as a Lambeth incident, but the site now sits in Southwark. Lambeth was hard pressed itself on 16/17 April; 223 of its citizens were killed. A plaque now marks the spot of Walklin's Bakery by the Young Vic.

Camberwell didn't have a 'major' incident as in the magnitude of Walklin's Bakery, but all parts of the borough had incidents and loss of life; forty-five were killed in the borough, from Burbage Road in the south to Bethwin Road in the north, on the border with Southwark. In Edinburgh Mansions, Bethwin Road, three members of the Trout family lost their lives. Part of the area was designated as slum dwellings before the war and underwent a massive rebuild after the war, with much social housing being built in the 1950s and 1960s.

At 2.15 a.m. on 17 April, a landmine descended on Talfourd Road, not far from Camberwell's town hall and control centre. Despite the large explosion, only three were killed. Earlier, in neighbouring Lyndhurst Way, eight were killed as a high-explosive demolished several houses. One of those killed was Albert Froud, whose highly respected family had a local haulage company, Henry Froud Ltd. Much of their fleet was used in war work in the borough.[iv]

Away went the Luftwaffe in the early hours of 17 April. For those emerging from their shelters, particularly in Southwark, their ever-changing vista had changed again; more buildings had been destroyed and more loved ones had been killed or injured.

The Luftwaffe did call again on 19 April – not with the severity of two days earlier, but still a raid of some size. Rotherhithe particularly bore the brunt of the many incendiary bombs dropped. Rotherhithe Street and surrounding streets were quite heavily peppered. Damage was recorded as light in general, and nobody in Bermondsey lost their life.

Ethel Peacock, from Southwell in the Midlands, had worked for the St Olave's District Nursing Association and was based at the nursing home at Cherry Garden Street. Ethel, who was training as a Queen's District Nurse, set off from Cherry Garden Street to visit an expectant mother, Mrs Louisa Ludgrove, in Renforth Street. Her colleagues were sheltering in the nursing home cellar, but they made sure Ethel had a strong cup of tea before she set off on her five-minute cycle ride.

Ethel arrived at the property in Renforth Street as the raid was intensifying; she had already seen incendiary bombs find their mark on buildings along the route. She was greeted by an Air Raid Warden, a Mr Walker, who suggested that they should evacuate the property immediately, particularly as the block of flats Mrs Ludgrove lived in had caught fire. However, the patient was in a serious condition as birth was imminent. Other residents of the block had left for the local shelter.

A baby girl, Lillian, was born at 10.30 a.m. the following morning; Ethel had been tending to and comforting her patient all night. Just as Lillian was born, there was a knock on the flat door. A policeman was at the door, ordering them out as an unexploded bomb was about 100 yards away and was liable to explode. Ethel explained that Louisa and Lillian couldn't be moved; instead, she put her arm across mother and child to shield them from any blast. The bomb exploded, lifting the bed off the floor, but the building held firm and all three survived. Ethel Peacock went on with her midwifery career, working as tutor of midwives at the nursing home, winning a succession of awards for her skill in her chosen field.

An almost three-week lull in the raids made London a cheerier place to be, but there was more to come. With Germany's invasion of Russia imminent, Hitler wanted to give London a farewell gift, the gift being a raid bigger than the April raids; the night was 10/11 May 1941. One warden at Peek Frean's biscuit factory remarked, 'We knew we were going to get it that night!'

The Luftwaffe approached Bermondsey, Camberwell and Southwark towards midnight on the 10th. A big target was the major junction of the Elephant and Castle; with the amount of incendiary bombs ploughed into it, the Elephant was on fire. The Surrey Theatre in Blackfriars Road had been closed since the mid-1930s and the building had been destroyed in earlier raids. Now the theatre had another use – the cellar was being used as an emergency water supply tank. The water from this tank was to be used to fight the fires at the Elephant and Castle. Hoses had been laid down and connected. Just as seventeen firemen were connecting their hoses to the water supply, a high-explosive bomb hit the building and all seventeen were killed. Most of the firemen were from Lee Green and Downham fire stations. Ironically, leading fireman James Johnson lived in Crampton Street at the Elephant and Castle. A blaze was raging out of control between Newington Butts and Crampton Street near his home.

Arthur Cross lived with his young family in Douglas Buildings, Marshalsea Road, near Borough underground station. Known to all as Harry, he had won the Victoria Cross in the First World War with the Machine Gun Corps in 1918 at Ervillers, France. His Victoria Cross was used for the film *Carrington V. C.*, starring David Niven.

Harry's young family was his second family. With his First World War experiences and trench warfare, Harry refused to go into confined spaces like an air-raid shelter. Therefore, he settled his family into the Douglas Buildings air-raid shelter and went off fire-watching.

The Southwark Air Raid Wardens' log for 11 May 1941 reported, 'Shelter hit. People trapped. Rescue Party at work. Some bodies recovered. 4 casualties sent to hospital. All bodies recovered; 4 females, 1 female child, 1 male child.'

The female child was Mary Cross, aged three, and the male child was Terence Cross, aged five. One of the females was Minnie Cross. Harry had lost his young family and was not killed himself because of his demons from the First World War.

The irony of Harry's loan of his Victoria Cross for *Carrington V. C.* was that the press coverage reunited him with his sister Diana in Norfolk, who thought that he had perished along with his family. Harry died in 1965 and is remembered in Streatham Vale Cemetery. For his funeral, his neighbours had a wreath made in the shape of a Victoria Cross. Harry hadn't wanted a headstone, but one was erected in 2001 in remembrance of the family and Harry's first wife.

Superintendent Robert Briggs of Southwark Police Station was a busy man. The roof of the married quarters of the station was set alight by a shower of incendiary bombs. Briggs and other officers from the station organised a relay of buckets of water to be fed up to the roof until the blaze was extinguished.

The LCC Weights and Measures Office in nearby Harper Road took a direct hit from a landmine. Despite his exhausting endeavours at the police station, on hearing there were people trapped, Briggs set off for the incident.

On arrival, he immediately climbed on to the debris and shouted for signs of life of those trapped. He heard moans but was unable to find his way in, so he sought another. The raid was still at its height and bombs were falling with regularity in the vicinity; a shower of incendiary bombs hit the debris, setting some of it alight. This new blaze had to be extinguished, so he called to two women to bring water from neighbouring houses. Having brought the fire under control, Briggs set about locating the trapped. He made contact with a man pinned down by masonry and ascertained there were ten people trapped. Further police assistance arrived along with the rescue service, and Briggs was able to direct them to the location of the trapped people. Unfortunately, only two people were brought out alive, with thirteen dead.

Young Jack Dabbs lived with his mother and elder sister in Cromwell Buildings, Redcross Way, near Southwark Street. Sixteen-year-old Jack was a messenger boy for the BBC and a messenger for the local Wardens' Post. The railway line from London Bridge station to Waterloo East runs across the northern end of Redcross Way. A high-explosive bomb burst through the railway arch and exploded near the Cromwell Buildings shelter. The gas main burst as did the water mains. Panic was beginning to set in within the shelter as water began seeping in and the gas main started leaking. Post warden Lesson's wardens were heavily involved at other incidents in the area. Lesson turned to young Jack and instantly promoted him to warden.

Jack immediately instilled an air of calm to the beleaguered shelterers; he carried youngsters across to Borough High Street and directed them with their mothers down to the deep shelter at The Borough. Even when a high-explosive bomb fell just yards from him, Jack was a model of coolness and bravery. He continued his escort duties through the night and earned immense praise from Lesson.

All parts of Southwark suffered with the intense bombing; not a corner of the borough was spared. In the west of the borough, a single incendiary bomb was responsible for the destruction of St George's Roman Catholic Cathedral. The entire building was ablaze from end to end within minutes and was a smouldering ruin by the following morning. The Amigo Hall was used for services thereafter. The rebuilding was not completed until 1958. Considering the magnitude of the building, appeals were sent out across the globe to supplement the war damage grant.

St Paul's Church, Lorrimore Square, stood just off Walworth Road in the heart of working-class Southwark. Several incendiary bombs lodged in the church roof and set light to the timbers; the church was soon ablaze. By morning, all that remained were the tower and the vestries. Father Royle, the vicar of the church, wrote in the parish magazine, 'For those who loved St Paul's, but not our Lord, the loss is unlimited, but for those who love our Lord, the lost may even be turned to gain.'

The wardens of reporting Post 12 were not having a good time, like most of the others posts in Southwark. It seemed as if they and their fire marshal colleagues were running from fire to fire, but still the sky glowed. They reported that the fire service was not to be seen. The post estimated that over 2,000 incendiary bombs fell in their post area alone – too many to record individually in the Wardens' log. High-explosive bombs fell too. One fell on the junction of Manor Place and Stopford Road, completely demolishing Carter's Newsagents and Tobacconists. A glass case from Griffiths' Dairy was blown completely across the road, landing in the Surrey Gardens Hotel. The rescue services came to the fore again at this incident, rescuing two trapped people.

The fire at the Elephant and Castle was still raging as the water supply was dwindling. The fire was consuming the north end of Walworth Road, Newington Butts, St George's Road, New Kent Road, Borough Road and London Road – a huge expanse of land. The fire service was powerless to deal with fires as there was an absence of water. All they could do was hack away at shopfronts and wooden hoardings to try and prevent the spread of the fires. A further casualty in the Post area was the church of St Mary, Newington, falling prey to the merciless incendiary bombs. The tower remains to this day along with an arch as a reminder to this night.

Southwark had certainly had a time of it during this night, but they were not alone in their strife.

Albert Henley was a man of the people and also the Mayor of Bermondsey, a staunch trade unionist and tireless worker in the dark days of 1940 and 1941. He lived with his wife Gladys at their home in Drummond Road in the very heart of Bermondsey. Peak Frean's biscuit factory was also in Drummond Road, and many employees there were his friends.

During his term of office, he worked tirelessly for his people and would often sleep in his office at the town hall. He was never slow to support worthy causes such as food supplies for those bombed out or clothing for those who had lost everything. A bout of pneumonia kept him out of his office for only ten days in the winter.

During the day of 10 May, he and Gladys had been over to watch a rehearsal of the play *Journey's End*, written by R. C. Sherriff; the play was set in the trenches in the First World War at the Clubland church. They also attended a fund-raising event at a youth club in Rotherhithe New Road.

As the evening's raid began to build up, he and his brother had already helped remove a piano off a man in a bombed house and had removed incendiary bombs off the roof of the Electricity Board building behind the town hall complex in Neckinger. Henley then returned to his office in the town hall to catch up with some paperwork. His chauffeur, Eddy Taylor, knocked on his door to tell him that Peak Freen's shelter had been hit. 'I'm coming,' was Henley's reply. He left his lucky jumper in his office. As he stepped into Spa Road to be driven to Peek Frean's, a high-explosive bomb landed close by and the Mayor of Bermondsey was fatally wounded; he died in St Olave's Hospital later in the day.

Bermondsey, much like Southwark, took a hammering; the Wardens' log is like an A–Z of Bermondsey street names, repeated many times over. The first reported bombs were a stick of incendiaries falling across Rotherhithe Street just before midnight on the 10th. Wichelow's leather factory in Riley Road was soon hit, and rescue services acted swiftly to try and free three people trapped. The rescue work was in vain as two fire-watchers were discovered dead when they were dug out later on the 11th.

The first recorded deaths were in Grange Road at 00.35 a.m.; Sophia Brown and her two-year-old daughter, Alice, were the victims, along with Clara Austin. Twenty people were trapped in Martin Crescent; seven were killed, including fireman Alma Harvey and his daughter.

The death toll was beginning to mount up as one o'clock in the morning became two o'clock.

The Southwark Park Estate and Southwark Park Road were subject to a fierce number of high-explosive and incendiary bombs. One of Elsie 'Chick' Payne's friends and fellow Girl Guide from St James's church, Vera Titchener, aged fourteen, and her mother were killed at their home at No. 80 Southwark Park Road. Honoria Sullivan and her son, Terence, were killed at No. 78 next door.

Fifteen people were injured as a high-explosive bomb landed opposite the Colleen Bawn public house at the eastern end of Southwark Park Road. Another public house, the Star and Windmill in Bermondsey Street, was demolished, with several people killed. Also in Bermondsey Street, Warden Fred Creasy was killed when a wall collapsed on him while he was searching for a missing child.

No part of the borough was a safe place to be; the destruction was horrific. Barrow, Hepburn and Gale in the Grange lost 80 per cent of their floor space on this night. Peak Freen's lost 40,000 square feet of factory space, but through the supreme effort of the workforce, the factory was up and running ten days later.

Camberwell, along with Bermondsey and Southwark, was subjected to a frightening ordeal. The very north of the borough, where Burgess Park is now, is home to a variety of activities ranging from sports pitches to families and friends enjoying their leisure time. In the pre-war years there were housing and industry, including R. White's drink factory in Cunard Street. Several high-explosive bombs found their mark in the street; sixteen people died in the small rows of terraced houses, including husband and wife Air Raid Wardens George and Agnes Parsons.

As with Bermondsey and Southwark, fires were apparent across Camberwell. Behind the public baths in Camberwell Green, fires were spreading into the yard of the cartage company in Harvey Road, owned by a Mr Beadle. The yard contained a 1,000-gallon petrol tank and two lorries, one of which was ablaze.

Employee and local fire-watcher Charlie Smith was aware of what was happening. Instantly he ran into the yard and drove the lorry which was not on fire, containing several tons of cotton, out of the yard, thus blocking the burning lorry. Charlie hurried back into the yard, started up the burning lorry and drove it away from the rear to a safe location. Another company employee, Mr Harrison, commented that Charlie's brave action had saved the yard and more than likely, Camberwell Baths.

Fire-watcher Walter Murton lived in St George's Way, which skirts the modern Burgess Park to the south. An oil bomb fell on his neighbour's house, home to

Mr and Mrs Allen. The couple were trapped in the basement kitchen with fire raging. Walter was swift to act; seeing that the only access was through a small window to the kitchen, he smashed it and ripped out the window frame. He was able to pull Mr Allen through the gap made. With the fire increasing in intensity both men pulled Mrs Allen to safety despite her clothes being on fire.

Walter then gave first aid to the couple, who were both burnt, then took them a nearby shelter from which they were conveyed to the hospital.

Camberwell Wardens' Post No. 46 was in Athenlay Road, Nunhead, in the very south of the borough and was also locally known as the 'Early Post'. A short walk across the railway bridge nearby would take one into neighbouring Lewisham. The post warden was Reverend Francis Tolley, the vicar of the local Silas' church.

A high-explosive bomb found its mark in Athenlay Road in the early hours of the morning of 11 May, killing the reverend and five of his wardens. The nearby St Silas' church was also damaged. Despite the incident being in Camberwell, all six bodies were taken to Lewisham Hospital; therefore, they were recorded as Lewisham casualties. Francis Tolley had been the vicar of St Silas' for two years, and his funeral was held under the shattered roof of the church four days later.

Bournemouth Road in heart of Peckham is close to the shops in Rye Lane and Peckham Rye Station. The neat little terraced street had surface shelters to supplement the Anderson shelters some residents had.

At 1.45 am on 11 May, two high-explosive bombs fell in quick succession, killing seventeen people and injuring many more.

Stretcher-bearer Charles Cozens and his party were helping a 'shock' victim into an ambulance as the bombs fell in Bournemouth Road. All received a nasty shaking as they were thrown to the ground and were covered in dust and debris.

They safely returned to their depot, supposedly to rest, but as another call came; as there were no other available parties to attend, they set off for Dowlas Street. A bomb exploded near their car as they were travelling along Southampton Way, bursting a tyre. When they got to their destination, the call turned out to be a false alarm. So back they went to the depot. As they turned into Rye Lane, a shower of incendiary bombs fell, several hitting the car roof.

When they arrived at the depot, it was another quick turnaround as they were sent to Windsor Walk at the top of Denmark Hill. This time there were casualties at the scene, who were taken to the nearby King's College Hospital.

Finally, Charles Cozens and his party could put their feet up and rest after a perilous night's work.

A bewildered Blitz-scarred public emerged from their shelters wondering how much more could they take. How many air raids of this magnitude could London take? Fate was about to take another twist; Hitler's dream of taking on the Red Army in search of 'Lebensraum' was in the wind. There were air raids, but these were like a pebble dropping into a pond rather than the boulders of 16/17 April and 10/11 May. On 23 May, the *South London Press* was moved to headline the words, 'Where's the Luftwaffe?' Also, other British newspapers were urging the United States to come into the war. Their wish came true following the Japanese bombing of Pearl Harbor on 7 December.

On 22 June 1941, the German army cranked up their Panzers and off went the Luftwaffe into Soviet skies as the ill-fated Operation Barbarossa began.

Londoners were even thinking about rebuilding their shattered lives. More goods were returning to high-street shops, and as early as the summer of 1941, there were initial talks concerning the rebuilding of London.

Weapons and salvage drives were aplenty in the capital, with boys' clubs, the Scouts and other youth organisations trying to collect the most of the latter.

What Britain needed was some kind of victory, but this was not to come until May 1943 in north Africa.

By the end of 1941 there was hope. Perhaps this hope can be summed up by Reverend Francis Tolley in his last words in St Silas' church before his death, 'We are all in this struggle together for the freedom of the human spirit and let us get together with the spirit of God.'

Damage to Barrow, Hepburn and Gayle's Factory on 11 May 1941. (Southwark Local Studies Library)

Mayor Albert Henley, killed outside Bermondsey Town Hall on the night of 10/11 May 1941. (Southwark Local Studies Library)

Local children gaze at a destroyed air-raid shelter on the Neckinger Estate. (Southwark Local Studies Library)

Volunteers making sandwiches at a rest centre. (Southwark Local Studies Library)

Covered-up entrance to an air-raid shelter on the Stansfeld Estate, Dunton Road. (Author's collection)

Destroyed air-raid shelter in Glengarry Road, Peckham. (Southwark Local Studies Library)

Camberwell control centre in the Town Hall. (Southwark Local Studies Library)

A Camberwell civil defence unit prepares for a hard night's work. (Southwark Local Studies Library)

Memorial plaque to the firemen killed at the old Surrey Theatre on 10/11 May 1941. (Author's collection)

A grainy photo of the old Surrey Theatre, destroyed in 1940, where seventeen firemen lost their lives. (Southwark Local Studies Library).

Nos 8–10 Skipton Street in the early twentieth century. Over twenty people were killed on 16/17 April 1941. (Southwark Local Studies Library)

A view from one of Guy's Hospital buildings towards the city in 1941. (Southwark Local Studies Library)

Above: The remains of St Mary Newington are a stark reminder to the last night of the 'Night Blitz'. (Author's collection)

Opposite: Memorial stone of Arthur 'Harry' Cross VC in Streatham Vale Cemetery and remembrance of his wife and two children who were killed at the Borough on 10/11 May 1941. (Author's Collection)

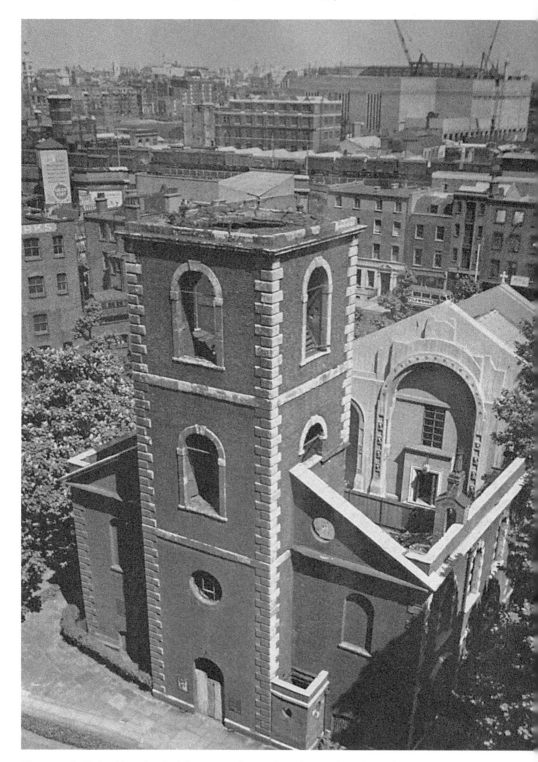

The gutted Christ Church, Blackfriars Road. (Southwark Local Studies Library)

The modern-day Christ Church, Blackfriars Road. (Author's collection)

Following the destruction of Christ Church, Blackfriars Road, Southwark Council, paved the spot where the church's burning cross fell. (Author's collection)

1942 and 1943
The Middle Years

The Night Blitz had effectively been over since May 1941. Nuisance raids did occur. The threat of invasion was still on people's lips, but the mood of the country was changing to a more relaxed one. Civil personnel were restless; there was very little for them to do.

There was concern of a 'blackout lull'. On 14 April 1942, a *South London Press* reporter reported that chinks of light from premises in Southwark were a common occurrence, particularly from pubs. It was said that the light from a cigarette could be seen from 3 miles up in the sky. A Mr Powell of Dulwich reported that at least half a dozen houses in Court Lane were showing chinks of light, and the same was being repeated in surrounding streets and wondered where wardens or the police were.

Local papers started to publish photos of group of captured service personnel now resident in the 'Stalags', with appeals for identification.

With the end of the Night Blitz, families started filtering back towards their native cities. Again, problems were mounting for them and the authorities. There was bad news for families returning to Camberwell; many had stored their property with a depository in Farquhar Road on the border with Lambeth, Lewisham and Croydon, only to find that the place had been ransacked and their goods were gone.[i]

Despite Russia's rumblings and with the United States only having been on the war for a few months, there was no sign of a second front in Western Europe. There was massive support for Council and privately generated 'weapons drives'. In 1942, 'Warship Week' was 21–28 March. Southwark's target was to raise £700,000 for the destroyer HMS *Quentin*. Bermondsey's goal was a similar figure for HMS *Quadrant*, likewise Camberwell for HMS *Penn*.

Southwark squeezed over the finishing line by £1,000; Camberwell boasted, 'We've bust it!'as a staggering £850,000 was raised, and Bermondsey's return was a rollicking £22,000 over their target.[ii]

Leaping ahead temporarily to 1 December 1942, HMS *Quentin* with four ships of Force 'Q', HMS *Aurora*, HMS *Argonaut,* HMS *Serius* and HMAS *Quiberon* (Australian) were tasked with intercepting an Italian/German convoy sailing from Palermo to Bizerte.

The attack on the convoy on the night of 2 December was highly successful with four freighters and one destroyer being sunk; two other destroyers received severe damage. The Allied force received no damage.

Returning to their base at Bone the following morning, Force 'Q'came under attack from a force of German torpedo bombers, followed by a formation of thirteen Junkers Ju-88s. *Quentin* was hit by a 500-kilo bomb and sank in four minutes; twenty crew members died and the remainder were transported away by *Quiberon.*

The MP for North Southwark, George Isaacs, said, 'We regret the loss of the *Quentin*, but knowing the glorious fight she put up, we can be proud of her. Her action when she went down still with her guns firing brings reflected glory to the Borough of Southwark.'

Still on a naval theme, a popular Rotherhithe vicar, Reverend John Palmer, received the Distinguished Service Cross. He was the vicar at St Katherine's church, Eugenia Road. He was known for his love of music, both classical and modern. In 1939 he composed 'The Rotherhithe Roll', a highly popular tune with the youngsters attending youth club dances. He was also well known for his broken and out-of-shape nose, a trophy as an amateur boxer in his youth.

Sadly, St Katherine's was destroyed by enemy action on 7 September 1940. The reverend answered the call to the colours to become a Navy Chaplain, winning his medal for 'bravery, endurance and sustained devotion to duty on His Majesty's ships Aurora, Acton Vale, Lance, Legion and at Malta during and after passage of an important convoy'.

Many shopkeepers would exhibit parts of bombs or planes that had been shot down in their windows, which were usually draped in patriotic slogans and national flags, encouraging patrons and passers-by to part with a few pennies or shillings for the war effort.

Elsewhere in Britain, other cities experienced the 'Baedekker Raids' from April to June 1942. The raids were a reprisal of the Bomber Command's bombing and near destruction of Lübeck in Northern Germany, a historic Hanseatic port. Incendiary bombs made very light work of the wooden buildings and structures. Around 1,000 people were killed in the inferno.

The Luftwaffe were using the famous Baedekker travel guides to select their targets. Over 1,600 people were killed in the raids, with over 1,750 injured. However, with the improvement and ferocity of anti-aircraft defences, the Luftwaffe paid a heavy price for their 'dip' into the famous guidebooks.

Gurney Street was a small street that ran from the New Kent Road to Deacon Street, a stone's throw from Elephant and Castle. There had been only one incident of note that affected the street in 1940/41; on 17 September 1940 a high-explosive bomb landed close by and the resulting fire damaged some property.

The Southwark Post 8 Wardens' log recorded a high-explosive bomb landing in Gurney Street on the last night of the Night Blitz, 11 May 1941, but 'services not required'. Following the raid, which had been particularly heavy in the area and across London, the Bomb Census authorities determined that a 50-kg bomb had exploded in the street and that was that.

6 June 1942 was a long, hot summer's day. Young children were just finishing up a game of cricket in the street; neighbours were chatting in doorways. The serenity of the evening was shattered at 9.30 p.m. when a thunderous explosion erupted; the noise was heard 5 miles away.

There was fury as to why the unexploded bomb had lain undetected for nearly thirteen months. Following an enquiry, Southwark MP Tom Naylor was given an 'explanation' by Mr Mabane, Parliamentary Secretary to the Ministry of Information. The statement was that the explosion was because a bomb dropped in May 1941 had wrecked a house, this bomb buried under the adjoining premises. He added that there was no evidence to suggest that there was an unexploded bomb *in situ*.

Could this explosion have been prevented? Mr D. C. Jones of Gurney Street stated on inspecting the damage afterwards that it was possible to trace the course of the bomb as it sliced its way into the ground floor, as it had left a neat round hole.

On being interviewed by an official, Mr Jones said that his examination had been from the pavement of the house. He had not informed the Civil Defence or the police of his suspicions. When asked if he felt any fear in living so close to a spot that was suspected to contain an unexploded bomb, he replied that he was living some distance away and, anyway, he preferred the opinion of the experts to his own.

Despite there obviously being no air-raid warning, the Ambulance Service was on the scene within several minutes, followed quickly by the rescue services. Light and heavy rescue services from Camberwell worked hand in hand with their Southwark counterparts. Parliament gave high praise to the work of the Civil Defence Services at the incident. Possibly none worked as hard as fourteen-year-old Johnny Wallow, son of the landlord of the nearby Grosvenor Arms. Local resident Mrs Daley spoke of young Johnny, 'He worked from Saturday evening, right through the night until Sunday evening. He asked for a cup of tea, lay down for twenty minutes then was up again with the rescuers.'

Following official inspection of the blitzed site, the Ministry of Home Security (Research and Experiments Dept), it was concluded that the bomb which exploded was a 'G' Mine, a 1,000 lb mine (Bombenmine BM 1,000) that could be used at sea or could be dropped on land targets from the air. It could be dropped with or without parachute. Fragments of the bomb, blast effects and inspection of the crater all pointed to this type of bomb.

As to the cause of the explosion, no explanation was given. However, there had been quite a lot of demolition and repair work going on in the area; obviously, heavy machines and pneumatic drills were being used. Could the vibration of this type of machinery have stirred the mine from its slumber?

The death toll at Gurney Street was eighteen killed, including six children under the age of ten. Sixty-two people were seriously injured and seventy-two slightly injured. One of those killed was a well-known local character, Frank Shaw Dawson. Originally from the Gold Coast, Shaw had been a merchant navy stoker, a boxer in fairground booths, East Street tipster and street vendor. He was forty-three years old.[iii]

Bermondsey had three special visitors in November 1942: Red Army sniper Lyudmila Pavlichenko accompanied by Senior Lieutenant V. Ptchelintseff and Lieutenant N. Krasavchekno. Lyudmila had over 100 kills to date in the Russian campaign. All three Soviets wanted their photograph taken in the Town Hall under the photo of Alfred Henley, whom they deemed a 'hero of the Blitz'.

They gave the following statement of Anglo-Soviet solidarity:

With the people of Great Britain we are ready to claim justice for the destruction of London and the destruction of Sevastopol.[iv]

For the citizens of the Camberwell and Bermondsey, 1943 began with 'nuisance' raids in January.

Despite a huge barrage put by anti-aircraft batteries, on the night of 17/18 January German raiders got through and hit the streets of Camberwell. There was also criticism that the air-raid sirens had sounded after the first bombs fell.

Camberwell was hit in a variety of locations, but not with the intensity of 1940 and 1941. Forty-two incidents were recorded in the borough Wardens' Log.

Local Dulwich resident Corrinne Wakefield recalled in a Dulwich Society Newsletter that a terrific explosion was heard in the Playfield Crescent, Lytcott Grove and Melbourne Grove areas as a high-explosive bomb found its mark. Seven people were killed in Lytcott Grove and four in Playfield Crescent. At No. 9 Lytcott Grove, mother and daughter Ethel and Winifred Roberts were two of the victims, as were husband and wife, Evan and Lily Evans, at their home in Playfield Crescent.

The famous Peckham department store on the corner of Rye Lane and Hanover Park, Jones and Higgins, was hit in the raid, resulting in a fire and the deaths of two people, including seventy-one year-old fire-watcher George Parker.

Nearby to Jones and Higgins, the Rye Lane Baptist Chapel was badly damaged and remains unusable. This was the second tragedy for the pastor and Mrs Bamber – on 7 July 1940, their only son, Christopher, a pilot officer in the RAF, was killed. He was serving with 15th Squadron and was killed as his Blenheim crashed on a reconnaissance mission. His plane came down in Belgium, and he is buried in Bruges General Cemetery.

On 20 January 1943, the raid on Camberwell was followed by a lone raider dropping his payload at the junction of Plough Way, Lower Road and Rotherhithe New Road. A public house, the Red Lion Hotel, and the Midland Bank on Lower Road were two of the buildings badly hit.

Midland Bank clerk Joan Tipling was on duty that day and recalls,

> I never thought I should be here. I remember falling into space. I prayed aloud that I might be saved. Then I heard people moving about on the debris and it sounded as if they were merely scratching about. I heard someone call 'Ted' and shortly afterwards I felt air coming through.
>
> I prayed aloud again and then a hand came through the opening and it cleared the dirt away from my mouth and then put a cup of warm sweet tea to my lips so I could drink. I begged the owner of the hand not to leave me because I felt I should be lost for good if he did.
>
> My life was undoubtedly saved by 'Ted'. He cupped my head in his hand and cleared the way for me to be saved.[v]

Not as fortunate as Joan at the bank was Home Guard Lieutenant Sydney Hutton, who lost his life along with fourteen others in the vicinity.

During 1943, shelter vandalism was a problem for the authorities as was shelter theft. Doors of shelters were often locked by shelter marshalls, which made the shelters practically useless if a raid was on and there was nobody immediately available to unlock them.

Wardens went into schools to 'enlist' the help of school children, urging them not to steal from or damage shelters, also report anyone else doing to the police or wardens' service. One Camberwell warden delivered quite a thought-provoking talk to a group of school children. 'A traitor is a man working against his own country. In wartime a man is shot for that. Yet there are many people and some children stealing electric lamps and destroying fittings inside air raid shelters who go unpunished. They are making it impossible to leave shelters unlocked because of their dishonesty.'[vi]

Bermondsey Council came up with a plan to combat shelter vandalism, offering a shield for the cleanest shelter in the borough. It was estimated that over 2,000 electric light bulbs had been stolen in one night alone.

April 1943 brought further 'nuisance raids' over south London; these were part reprisal for Allied bombing of Berlin and the Ruhr dams. Bigger raids took place in other parts of the UK, notably Cardiff and the north-east, particularly Sunderland.

Incidents were few and casualties in general light except in East Surrey Grove, where a Luftwaffe raider snuck in and dropped a 500 lb bomb on the street, killing fourteen and injuring thirty-five. Twenty houses were demolished with many others damaged.

A local post warden was on his beat on his cycle and was thrown by the blast. He remarked, 'I heard a plane circling overhead. It dived and made a run for some hundreds of yards towards a factory, releasing its bombs just over it.'

One of those killed was sixteen-year-old Joan Fowler. Joan would regularly sell tickets for charity dances, which were always in aid of the war effort. This week it was for the sick and wounded of the 8th Army.

Raffles and spot prizes were always popular at the events and Joan always bought tickets, but failed to win a prize. However, at this week's week dance she won her first prize, a ten-shilling note. Two hours after her win, Joan was dead.

The warden who ran the dances said, 'In the log book of our memories, Joan will always rank alongside the heroes who fell in Tunisia, because they were last in her thoughts.' Joan's parents, Ethel and John, were also killed.

Like the raids earlier in the year, bombs were dropping before the warning sirens sounded. Councillor George Loveland of Bermondsey was adamant that the warning sirens were inadequate.

The family of the Mayor of Southwark, A. J. Gates, had some warming news as his nephew, Private Bill Gates, was mentioned in dispatches for his work in the Battle of El Alamein in the Western Desert.

May 1943 gave the public the victory they wanted. After much bitter fighting and see-sawing across the north African desert, German and Italian troops surrendered on 13 May.

In June 1943 a memorial service was held in memory of the citizens of Lidice, Czechoslovakia, murdered as scapegoats for the assassination of Reinhard Heydrich, the Nazi Controller of Bohemia and Moravia. In attendance was the Czech Foreign Minister Jan Masaryk. The service was held in Spa Road where Mayor Henley had been killed in May 1941.

The Foreign Minister thanked Bermondsey for the service and added, 'We shall destroy Hitler and we shall march into Berlin and then we shall take some Bermondsey manners to the Germans.'[vii]

With air raids very much scaled down, the LCC was drawing up its plans for the rebuilding of south London, including redeveloping the South Bank from County Hall to Waterloo and eastwards. The LCC was also proposing the 'Building a Career' scheme with the building industry in mind. Proposals included a wide range of careers within the industry with day, evening and weekend courses available.

Collections for the war effort on various fronts continued; with Anglo-Soviet aid at the fore, the landlord of the Brunswick Tavern in the Old Kent Road was urging his customers to part with their money with the promise that he would double their contributions weekly for this cause. Meanwhile, Bermondsey's Civil Defence personnel were setting out to raise funds for the St Dunstan's War Blinded charity.

The 'official' drive was 'Warplanes Week', with boroughs trying to secure the biggest collection of money. Out of this year's campaign came two well-known and iconic B-17 bombers for the United States Army Air Force: *Rotherhithe's Revenge* and *The Bermondsey Battler*.

Food rationing was still a feature of the middle-war years, but despite people not able to purchase food without them, in July 1943 over 6,000 books were unclaimed in south-east London.

Hop-picking in Kent and Sussex was the traditional holiday destination for working-class folk from south and south-east London. Trains from local railway stations were crammed with the hop-pickers and their families. 1943 was no different, but it also offered families the chance to have a country break, away from the scars of the Blitz.

The *South London Press* reported that this summer hop farms were offering incredibly high rates to their temporary employees; in some cases it was double the normal rate – one shilling for a basket of hops. Hop farm owners were inundated with postal requests, but stayed loyal to their regular south Londoners, adamant that these would be the first invited.

For those staying in London, the 'Holiday at Home' scheme was adopted, with many events being put on in large open spaces, such as Southwark Park.

In complete contrast to the news that the Mayor of Southwark, A. J. Gates, received earlier in the year, Councillor C. A. G. Manning, the ARP Controller of Southwark, received the worst kind. His son, Pilot Officer Cecil Walter Manning, was reported missing, piloting his Lancaster on an attack on Peenemünde on the raid of 17/18 August. The aircraft crashed off the coast of Denmark with no trace. Pilot Officer Manning had trained in South Africa and was in the Royal Air Force Volunteer Reserve for 12 Squadron, based at Wickenby. He lived in Wandsworth with his wife Muriel and their three children.[viii]

As a footnote to the Mannings' story, in 1944 Councillor Manning was elected as MP for North Camberwell. He was asked to resign his post as ARP Controller for Camberwell as the council thought he would not be able to fulfil both posts. This he did reluctantly, with the post going to his deputy.

The news of the Italian surrender on 8 September was a real boost for the nation, and on a lighter note an East Dulwich fish and chip shop owner – who ran out of stock one day in September – put up a notice in his window, 'ITALY'S SOLD OUT, SO AM I!'

There was a small raid on 18 October 1943, with very few bombs landing; most of the small amount of damage was done by anti-aircraft shells. One of these shells landed outside the Camberwell Home Guard drill hall. Major Burford and Private Best were injured; the latter required the amputation of two fingers after being struck by shrapnel.

With the closure of 1943, 1944 was certainly going to be one to remember for a variety of reasons.

Grave of Chris Dix in Camberwell New Cemetery, killed at his home in Lytcott Grove, East Dulwich, on the 'Tip and Run' raid of 17 January 1943. (Author's collection)

A very grainy photograph of the Rye Lane Baptist Chapel which had been gutted on 17 January 1943. (Author's collection)

THIS CHAPEL WAS SERIOUSLY
DAMAGED BY ENEMY ACTION
SUNDAY 17TH JANUARY 1943
IT WAS RE-OPENED FOR PUBLIC WORSHIP
SUNDAY 4TH JULY 1948

A plaque on Rye Lane Baptist Chapel reminding us of the chapel being hit. (Author's collection)

1944
Small and Large Packages

The 'Pearly Kings and Queens' of London are traditionally among the most buoyant and bubbly characters in the capital, always donating their time to charitable events and causes. Mary Tinsley was no different. In January 1944, the 'Pearly Queen' of Southwark was collecting money in the Elephant and Castle Theatre. She had lost her son Patrick in October 1943 during the Italian campaign. Patrick had been fighting with the Royal Irish Rifles and is buried in Bari War Cemetery. His last letter home to his parents contained the words, 'God bless Monty'.[i]

The Luftwaffe was back over south-east London in January, the start of the 'Baby Blitz'. Raiding was almost a shadow of what went before in 1940 and 1941.

On the raids of 21 and 22 January no serious incidents occurred in the three boroughs. The first major incidents were in Camberwell on the 29th. Lives were lost in Marlborough Grove and Rolls Road,the intended target being the South-Eastern Metropolitan Gas Works in the Old Kent Road.

Casualties tended to be light through the February until the 20th. Between fifty and sixty raiders had crossed the coast and were heading towards London. As the Luftwaffe dropped their payload over Bermondsey, fourteen incidents were recorded in the Wardens' log, the most serious being in Thurland Road, where nine people were killed, including Air Raid Wardens Walter Hubbard and Sidney Johnson.

In Camberwell, seventeen people were killed as a bomb hit home on the junction of East Surrey Grove and Commercial Way, including nine-year-old Robert Simkins.

Southwark didn't escape this raid as a bomb struck Rephidim Street, just off Tower Bridge Road, killing four people, including a mother and daughter both named Mary Ann Sweeney.

It is noticeable again that a good percentage of damage was caused by anti-aircraft shells returning to earth. In some cases these shells were responsible for the deaths.

Raiding through March 1944 was restricted primarily to Camberwell. A raid on 2 March killed seventy-eight-year-old Joe Congdon at his home in Chesterfield Grove and eleven-month-old John Sargent at Whorlton Road.

More raids followed in late March, with a few casualties. On 22 March, John Hender was talking to his friend John Rickard outside the King's Arms public house in East Dulwich Road. Rickard recalls hearing the air-raid siren at around 10 p.m. A third unknown person was involved in the conversation. Following the wail of the siren Rickard went off to join his mother at their home. He reached St John's Church in Adys Road when he heard an explosion. He knew it was close but did not know the details until the following day when he went to call on his friend. John Hender was mortally wounded in the blast and died the following day in Dulwich Hospital. John Hender was fifteen and worked as a fire service messenger. Four other people were killed in East Dulwich Road.[ii]

The 'Baby Blitz', also known as 'Operation Steinbock', lasted from January to May 1944; in this period just over 1,500 people were killed with nearly 3,000 injured nationwide. Seven people were killed in Southwark, fifteen in Bermondsey and thirty-seven in Camberwell. The last casualty occurred in the least hit of the three boroughs, Southwark. On 10 May, Esther Grimwood was the victim in the Southwark part of the Old Kent Road.

An unsuspecting public were unaware of the horrors to come in the summer.

A curious story appeared in the *South London Press* in March 1944. Rifleman Charles Hampshire of Walworth had the habit of chalking south London pub names on captured buildings in the Western Desert. One of these was the famous 'Bricklayers Arms' in the Old Kent Road. A German prisoner of war was looking the chalk sign with much interest. When Hampshire quizzed him about his curiosity, the prisoner told him that he had been there many times in pre-war days.[iii]

D-Day, 6 June 1994, was broadcast to a startled public. The BBC began their announcements at 9.45 a.m. A German version was broadcast (in English) earlier with most listeners thinking this was an elaborate hoax.

Many factories kept the broadcasts going over their tannoys for the whole day, fearing that workers would not return from their lunch breaks, preferring to listen in local hostelries or their homes.

D-Day was greeted with much elation from a Blitz-weary public. To many people, this was the beginning of the end of German tyranny, not knowing that that victory was to be hard fought and costly in terms of service personnel, and indeed, many more lives would be lost on the Home Front.

The leader of the LCC, Lord Latham, erred on the side of caution when delivering a message following the D-Day landings. He said, 'On this historic day, when the liberation of Europe has begun, we at home must play our part. Our leaders have warned us that invasion may lead to fierce counter activity. The responsibility resting on you is great; your task might be heavy, but London looks to you with confidence.'

With the liberation of occupied Europe underway, it was now time for Germany to launch the first of their 'Vengeance Weapons'. With the Normandy invasion barely a week old, the first V-1s, commonly known as 'Doodlebugs', were launched at the capital.

Designed by Robert Lusser of the Fieseler factory, 9,251 were fired from the fixed launching sites on the Continent, with 2,515 reaching London. The range for the V-1 was up to 160 miles, the guidance system was a gyroscope-based autopilot. The warhead was amatol. With speeds up to 400 miles per hour, they were detectable, but difficult to pinpoint as they could be fired at any time, night or day.

The first notable strike was in Grove Road, Bethnal Green, on the night of 12/13 June, where the railway arch was struck. Among the victims was twelve-year-old Leonard Sherman. Initially, the early V-1 strikes were recorded in some Wardens' logs as 'PAC' or 'Pilotless Aircraft'.

The three boroughs didn't have to wait long for their turn to be hit; the first was a Camberwell incident on 15 June at the junction of Gibbon Road and Senate Road, almost on the border with Deptford. Four people were killed

Bermondsey's first incident was in the early hours of 16 June. Raymouth Road was hit just after midnight. Incident Officer Mr Julius initially reported three dead and twenty injured. The death toll rose to seven, and the blast demolished a number of houses.

A few hours later, at 5.25 a.m., another V-1 fell at the junction of St James's Road and Jamaica Road in the shadow of St James's church vicarage. All the windows of the church were shattered, and part of the ceiling was brought down. The church bells struck over 100 times then stopped, not to strike again until repaired after the war.[iv] People were sheltering in the coal cellar of the vicarage but were trapped in the debris from the blast. On the scene quickly were police constables Victor Bray and Frank Rudduck, along with local Wardens Frederick Florance and Edward Clark.

The vicar, Reverend Duckett, and several other shelterers were quickly rescued, but were informed that others were trapped, namely a Mrs Hatherley and her two daughters.

Police Superintendant Robinson arrived on the scene and set about coordinating the rescue of those still trapped. He, with Bray and Rudduck, went into the debris, where the three started making a tunnel. Meanwhile, at the rear of the building, the two wardens were trying to reach Mrs Hatherley's daughters. The rescue services had also arrived to add their support to the work, which was being carried out in very dangerous conditions with the buildings in imminent danger of collapse. The two policemen and the two wardens finally were able to release the trapped women.

Southwark's first visit from the new terror weapon was also on 16 June as the Waygood Otis lift factory, in Falmouth Road, took a direct hit. Ten people met their deaths in this incident, including some of the workforce who lived outside the borough.

It was not surprising that in the first eighty days of the V-1 strikes, Camberwell, given its respective size to Bermondsey and Southwark, was hit the most. However, with its large open spaces, particularly in the parks and sports fields of Dulwich, many early V-1s fell on such open spaces, such as Greendale, Dulwich Common and the Dulwich and Sydenham Golf Course, which was also an anti-aircraft battery site. It was not until 30 June that anyone was killed in the Dulwich area, when five people lost their lives in Underhill Road.

Bermondsey had seven V-1s delivered from 18 June to the end of the month, the most serious in terms of loss of life being on the 18th in the early hours of the morning when a V-1 hit Croft Street on the eastern end of the borough, almost in neighbouring Deptford. Nineteen people were killed or died from their injuries. Eight houses were destroyed, and there was significant blast damage in surrounding streets.

Harry Winter was away fighting with the Dorset Regiment in Normandy. It took a week for the news to filter to him that his mother and father, Lillian and Henry, had been killed by a V-1 that hit the air-raid shelter in Cancel Street, Walworth, on 19 June. Harry was given leave and he made it back to London for the funeral with very little time to spare. Neighbours Ada Shepherd and Hilda Gardner were also killed in the blast

Several V-1s that landed in Bermondsey towards the end of June fell on the Thames foreshore, with blast damage negligible to a degree.

Southwark was about to experience one of its worst incidents of the entire war on 19 June. On the corner of Great Guildford Street and Union Street there stood the Jolly Gardeners public house. Also in the same stretch of street was the King Henry VIII public house plus a variety of small businesses and light industries.

A good night was to be had by all in the Jolly Gardeners. One parishioner of the nearby Church of the Precious Blood was on his way to meet some friends, but decided to change his route, which made his journey longer. He was lucky as at just after 10 p.m. a V1 ploughed into the junction of Great Guildford Street and Union Street. Many people were in the cellar bar of the Jolly Gardeners. The explosion caused the walls of the pub to fall into the pub, an effect known as 'pancaking'. Hence all were trapped in the cellar. To seal their fate, the explosion burst a water main, which began to fill up the cellar. Forty-seven people died in the incident, many from drowning. The blast damage was severe in the vicinity. The blocks of flats built in the late 1930s opposite the site of the pub show blast damage and repairs. Today the area is vastly different from the 1940s. The Jolly Gardeners was rebuilt after the war, but has since been converted into offices as have many of the older buildings in this particular part of Southwark.

On the corner of Peckham Rye and Nunhead Lane, there stood W. S. Thompson, corset makers. Local resident Robert Gibbons can recall 22 June 1944 with special reason.

I worked as an audit clerk for a firm of City accountants on Basinghall Street. I was walking down Peckham Rye (East) on my way to work.

I was about 50 yards past the Roberts' Capsule Co factory on the corner of Soloman's Passage, then a doodlebug came over. The engine cut out and the two or three people near me stopped in their tracks and waited for the inevitable 'landing'. There was a terrific explosion; the doodlebug had landed on the corset factory.

I wonder why none of us dropped to the ground for protection? We just stood there.[v]

Twenty-three people were killed in the incident or died from their injuries; many were young female workers from the factory, some in their mid-teens.

The following day, Walworth had its first V-1 incident; ten people were killed as Carter Street was hit, including the ironically named William Carter.

The *South London Press* published to its readers' advice from Civil Defence staff what to do if a V-1 approaches.

Experience is teaching us in such areas that a big percentage of casualties come from flying glass which shoots off at an angle of about 45 degrees.

If these bombs should come into your vicinity don't look up at them, get away from them, and if you hear the engine shut off, drop flat on your face, covering yours ears with your hands.

It appears that this advice was heeded within the following months as injuries from flying glass were reported as less frequent.

The death rate in Peckham was higher towards the end of June; residential property was more compacted in the back streets of this part of Camberwell. Twenty-four people were killed from seven V-1 strikes between 23 June and the end of the month.

Central Camberwell had a big incident on 25 June as a V-1 landed in Hillingdon Street near the boundary with Lambeth. Five streets were damaged, and many of the dead were recorded as Lambeth casualties, having been taken to Lambeth hospitals or mortuaries.

Three days later, Bentley House on the Brunswick Park Estate, near Camberwell, took a direct hit; nineteen people were killed and the block was badly damaged. Bentley House was rebuilt after the war with brickwork evidently different from the other blocks on the estate.

After nearly three weeks of V-1 strikes, the ever-changing faces of Bermondsey, Camberwell and Southwark were changing yet again. These weapons could do untold damage, particularly in parts of the densely populated boroughs of London; and, of course, deaths were occurring. By the end of June 1944 the death tolls were as follows:

Bermondsey	28
Camberwell	77
Southwark	104

Southwark's tally was compounded by the very large incident in Union Street.

One South London Mayor commented, 'It's a new kind of warfare; silent and remorseless.'

An eyewitness in Dulwich described a V-1 incident as follows:

I saw and heard the bomb coming from a long way off. It was travelling very fast and fairly low and its exhaust smoke was plainly visible. It reached the peak of its flight right over my head, when suddenly the engine petered out and stopped.

It immediately dived steeply with the Blitz time whine of a HE, then exploded. The period between the engine stopping and it exploding was about fifteen seconds.[vi]

Indeed, there was more to come prompting evacuation to safer parts of the country.

Stuart Road and Reynolds meet at a 'V' as Peckham Rye fades away into the distance. Seventeen people were killed on 1 July as houses on this junction were the recipients of the new month's onslaught. The now-familiar tale of whole families being killed rang true once more. The area today is a rebuilt modern estate; however, neighbouring streets give a clue to what the area once looked like.

Eleven people were killed in two incidents in other parts of Peckham namely Radnor Road and Costa Street the following day. In the case of the latter, Frank Harris recalls,

A German doodlebug engine ran out of fuel somewhere over where I was living in Bellenden Road, where our back gardens backed on to the back gardens of Oglander Road, and when I looked out of our kitchen window on the ground floor I saw a rocket gliding above the rooftops of the houses opposite and immediately crouched down in a corner of the kitchen by a large washing machine and put my fingers in my ears.

When the explosion, came our ceiling kitchen plaster came down and I was engulfed in white dust, rather like being in a snow storm. I rushed into the back garden and watched a large cloud of black smoke, with papers swirling in the air coming from the area of McDermott Road at the junction of Waghorn Street.[vii]

After somewhat of a lull, it was Bermondsey's time again. On 1 July, a V-1 thundered into Gainsford Street, just off Tooley Street. Seventeen people met their deaths, primarily in Horsleydown Mansions.

In Camberwell Station Road, parallel to the railway running from Elephant and Castle to Denmark Hill, a V-1 strike on 3 July killed five people, including three members of the Nurse family. The rebuild on the exact spot is very evident, particularly from the railway.

Still, Dulwich was relatively quiet as open ground took most of the hits. Camberwell Old Cemetery in Forest Hill Road and Greendale were hit with no casualties. Several days on that was to change as three people were killed at the junction of Park Hall Road and Alleyn Road on 5 July. The modern buildings on this corner, including a newer version of the Alleyn's Head public house, are a reminder to this incident.

A more serious incident occurred in Woodvale, almost in neighbouring Lewisham. White Gables bore the brunt of the fourteen civilians killed in this incident on 6 July.

A small lull followed for the three boroughs, although five were killed from a strike in Clayton Road, Peckham, on the 7th. The Green family were killed at No. 55, including young Pauline Green, just twenty-two months old.

Surrey Docks fell victim to a succession of four V-1s between the 9th and the 12th. Centre Yard and Russia Yard were the recipients, but casualties were light although there was damage to the Redriff Estate from the Centre Yard strike.

On the 10th, the famous Dulwich College was hit; a variety of buildings were damaged and rebuilt after the war. The school, although evacuated in 1940, continued to function as a school following the return to London of pupils. The V-1 struck near midnight; fortunately the school is not a boarding school and nobody was killed.

Dulwich Fire Station near the junction of Court Lane and Lordship Lane was destroyed the following day. The modern new-built properties in the surrounding area are further evidence of this incident.

Parts of the three boroughs were living slightly charmed lives in the middle of July, but not so Bermondsey. On 12 July, the SS *Tristran* in Brunswick Yard, Surrey Docks, was in trouble, with several people killed on board including Norwegian Gustav Petersen, and Australian merchant seaman Eric Chilvers.

On 15 July, White's Grounds Estate along the railway line near Bermondsey Street felt the might and power of the V-1; three people were killed, with over fifty injured. Otto Shockley of Peckham was the sole person killed as a V-1 struck in Tower Bridge Road the following day.

The Seven Islands Leisure Centre is a popular spot for swimmers and keep-fit enthusiasts in today's Southwark. It is located on the corner of Gomm Road and Lower Road, sandwiched between Southwark Park and Surrey Docks. It was not such a popular spot on 18 July as four were killed in Henwood Street just off Gomm Road. Over 150 people received treatment at local first aid posts.

Walworth's first V-1 for several weeks hit home on 17 July at Suffield Road, a short distance from Kennington underground station and the border with Lambeth. A densely populated area was severely blasted, with nearly 200 properties destroyed or damaged. Like many incidents related in this book, the area is now a post-war modern estate. Seventeen people were killed here, including four-month-old Michael Elligott and twenty-two-month-old Francis Haine along with his mother. It was Walworth's last but one 'V' incident, but the most costly in terms of lives lost. Deputy Post Warden Pullen recorded that the seventeen bodies he had seen were the most he had seen from one incident.

Peckham was back in the front line on 19 July as two V-1s struck two and a half hours apart within a couple of hundred yards of each other. The first was in Woods Road where six were killed and the second was in McKerrell Road, a small street of housing that runs off Hanover Park. Eleven people were killed in several locations, including two employees of property company, Benjamin Bull and Co in Peckham High Street.

More of Britain's history felt the full force of the terror weapons as on 21 July the famous Dulwich Picture Gallery was hit. As with many museums and galleries in the capital, the majority of important works were removed from London. In Dulwich's case some 600 works had been taken away to safe storage. There was damage to some of the remaining 100 pieces of work, of which some had the potential to be restored. There was nobody killed at the incident, but damage to the gallery and some nearby buildings was quite bad.

The last V1s of any real substance landing the three boroughs this month were on 29 July. Several were killed on Peckham Rye, including local Police Constable Albert Shephard at the lido on the Rye.

Early August 1944 opened up with a quieter period for Peckham and Southwark. The first V-1s broke the summer sunshine on the 3rd. Bermondsey had several incidents of blast damage from V-1s striking other boroughs including one from Stepney across the Thames.

On the same day, East Dulwich was also in the firing line once more as six people were killed in their homes in Crystal Palace Road and Jardin Street.

On Bermondsey Wall stood the Montreal Granary in Duden's Wharf. The old warehouses were home to stocks of peanuts, grain and linseed. As the evening sun was starting to wane, at 6 p.m. the building was struck by a V-1. The old timber warehouses stood no chance and were soon ablaze.

Bermondsey incident officers, Wiseman and Fraser, were quickly on the scene, but nothing could be done for local Fire Guard George Legon, who was killed instantly. Fortunately, the workforce had left for home, hence the small casualty list.

The River Fire Service and the regular fire service were also quickly in attendance, throwing gallons of water on to the conflagration, and their services were required for almost a week.

Sadly for the adjacent Loftie Street, the pressure of water forced a massive amount of the warehouse's contents into the local properties and gardens. What was salvaged from Duden's Wharf was quietly scooted away to other locations in the borough. The devastating fire rendered many local buildings unsafe and were demolished later.

With the grain seeds flooding the local properties, the addition of water and linseed, Bermondsey soon had its own grain field which wasn't removed until around Christmas 1944. The whole place was particularly unsavoury as the sewers were clogged and the long, hot summer brought a host of flies, who thrived on the damaged area.

When cleared, the rotten grain was taken away and buried very deep under Hackney Marshes. The warehouse buildings were completely demolished, and the whole site was chemically treated.[viii]

Like most local high streets of the time, Lordship Lane was a very busy place, particularly on a late Saturday afternoon as shoppers were trying to get the best value out of the ration cards. The Cooperative store stood on the junction of Lordship Lane and Northcross Road.

At 4.45 p.m. on 5 August 1941 the area was rocked as a V-1 scored a direct on the store. Other buildings in the vicinity were badly blasted. Evidence is still visible on the site, with new-build properties abundant opposite the site of the Co-op and indeed the Co-op itself.

One quick-witted shopkeeper, on hearing the cry 'There's one over the top!', ran for the stairs at the back of his shop, just about reaching them as his shop was demolished. He was injured but lived to fight another day.

The rescue squads worked through the night, bringing out the dead and the injured. Floodlights and flares were used to assist the rescue workers. The damage made the work painstaking, compounded by the fact that it wasn't known who and how many people were in the Co-op, neighbouring shops and premises. When all had been done and the incident closed after several days, twenty-three had been killed and sixty injured, many seriously.

The Dulwich Society has had a plaque erected at the site of the incident, now a pharmacy and an undertaker.

The area sandwiched between Tooley Street and the railway running out of London Bridge was littered with, and to a degree still is, social housing, such as the Guinness Trust Estate in Snowsfields, which nestles behind what was the old Sarson's vinegar factory; its chimney is another former feature for those travelling into London Bridge from Kent and the suburbs.

At 3.54 a.m. on 6 August, the estate was rocked by a V-1 strike, resulting in sixteen deaths. Among those killed was Dunkirk veteran and keen sportsman, Able Seaman Harry Martin, who was home on leave. Two blocks of the estate were demolished, with a further four badly damaged. The rescue services were ably assisted by an American naval unit stationed nearby. Canadian Army Service Corps serviceman Lorne Graham lost his wife Ruth and his two-month-old daughter, also named Ruth, at the Snowsfields incident.

The following day five were killed in East Dulwich when the junction of Friern Road and Underhill Road was hit. The damage was on a large scale as is clearly evident with post-war housing dominating the area. One of those to die (from shock) was ninety-three-year-old Clara Child, the oldest person to lose their life due to enemy action in the three boroughs.

A narrow escape was had by the workforce in Courage Brewery's garage in Queen Elizabeth Street between Tooley Street and the Thames. At 7.46 a.m. on 11 August the garage took a direct hit from a V-1, approximately fifteen minutes before 'clocking on' time for the workforce. Two people, however, were killed in the blast, with one further person dying a day later in hospital.

While central Camberwell was having a quieter time in the middle of August, V-1s were striking Peckham and Dulwich.

Two people were killed at the junction of Ivydale Road and Inverton Road in Nunhead on 12 August. The following day, the same number were killed in Scylla Road.

Peckham's last V-1 of summer 1944 fell on the clubhouse of post-war amateur football club Nunhead FC; the clubhouse was destroyed, but there were no deaths.

A big blast damaged a range of properties in Forest Hill Road, Therapia Road and Mundania Road on 17 August. Warden Harold Davis was one of two people killed.

Yvonne Wakefield lived in Jennings Road, and she and her family attended the local Lordship Lane Baptist chapel. Her father was the carpenter/handyman for the chapel. She recalled 22 August, when a V-1 landed almost opposite the chapel. She went to the chapel where her father was inspecting the damage.

Pre-war there was a very pretty 'duck-egg' coloured ceiling, pale turquoise blue. On that were painted little silver and/or white stars, with some stars made to hang attached by a point of a star to the ceiling, giving an effect to the viewer of looking to the Heavens. There were also lovely glass light fittings (very art-deco). Each one I seem to remember had a silver (chromium) pole between the ceiling and the light fitting; the latter being a simulation of the planet, Saturn, with a glass ball at the centre with a ring of glass round it to simulate Saturn's rings.

When I arrived there was glass from these light fittings embedded in 'my Dad's' formerly beautiful pews and rubble from the ceiling everywhere. I went up into the pulpit, which had been a pretty design of wrought iron with a wooden rail round the top. I gashed my finger on a piece of glass when I touched the rail.

'The organ was full of rubble too, which distressed me, because I was taking piano lessons at the time and I had a little play on it when nobody was looking, before the damage.[ix]

There was blast damage around the area, and there is still one pre-fabricated house in situ almost opposite the chapel.

Bermondsey's last major incident of the summer was on the same day; a V-1 hit the back of the Purbrook LCC estate in Riley Road. Thirteen were killed and fifty-six injured. The Riley Road side of the estate took most of the impact of the blast, as is evidenced by a range of post-war new builds. The Tower Bridge Road side of the estate appears to have stood up to the blast; as with several other estates, shelter signs still remain in several places.

London had endured eleven weeks of V-1s. The damage was on a vast scale. It was estimated that blast damage from a V-1 strike could travel up to 300 yards. Camberwell had eighty-one V-1 strikes. Over 400 houses had been destroyed, nearly 750 were damaged beyond repair and over 3,000 very badly damaged but repairs were possible.

In early September 1944, Herbert Morrison stated that Germany had lost the 'Battle of London'. Little did Londoners know that something more sinister was to pay a call.

With the 'Battle of London' apparently over, the government was considering a relaxation of blackout restrictions, a move that caught local authorities by surprise.

Local authorities also called on the government to release building materials quickly. With winter just around the corner, it seemed likely that some families would have to live in properties that had not yet been repaired. Pressure was added by evacuees returning to the capital from mid to late August. Food shortages were also apparent, with long queues outside food centres, and many bakers were very quickly selling out of bread.

Staveley Road is a quiet suburban street in Chiswick, west London. It lies in the shadow of the grounds of Chiswick House. At 6.44 a.m. on 8 September 1944, the late summer tranquil air was broken by a terrific explosion; three people were killed, with others trapped and injured. Initially a gas explosion was blamed and this was the official line, but with another occurring in the Epping area, within moments rumours abounded. Naturally a host of military and government officials were on the spot within no time. Tests proved that this was a new secret weapon, but a complete press embargo was enforced for several months.

The V-2 was a long-range rocket and a completely different prospect from the V-1, which flew across the Channel at approximately 400 miles per hour. It was detectable, albeit not much notice could be given, particularly at night. The V-2 could reach speeds of 3,500 miles per hour and was over the UK in minutes. With the speed, combined with 1,000-kg amatol warhead, the result would be devastating. The project was developed under the stewardship of Werner von Braun, who fell into the grateful arms of the Americans at the end of the war and went on to work on NASA's space programme.

An uneasy September 1944 disappeared with the autumn leaves. The first half of October had almost slid away when Nunhead got a reminder that the 'Battle of London' was not over. Surprisingly, it was not a V-2 that hit home but a V-1. The junction of Athenlay Road and Fernholme Road was hit on 15 October. Blast damage was considerable. Eight people were killed, including Warden Albert Axford in St Silas's church hall, the church where Warden Reverend Tolley and comrades were killed in 1941.

The first V-2 to hit home in the three boroughs was in Bermondsey. The John Bull railway arch crosses Southwark Park Road in an area known locally as the 'Blue', in reference to the nearby Blue Anchor public house. The V-2 struck the arch at 8.40 a.m. on 26 October. Fortunately,the resulting fires in the John Bull public house and Harvey and Thompson's pawnbrokers were quickly dealt with. Considering the location, which contained shops, housing and industry, very few were killed; only eight. However, over 100 people were injured, which is testimony to the ferocious destructive power of the V-2.

It was Dulwich's turn next as death came out of the early morning darkness on 1 November as at 5.15 a.m. Etherow Street and Friern Road got a rude awaking.

The number of people killed here (twenty-four) was to be the most killed in a V-2 incident within the three boroughs. All of the deaths occurred in Friern Road; among the dead were eight-month-old Pauline Lomas along with her mother Elsie. Again, the blast caused serious damage, with the area totally rebuilt.

Guy Fawkes' Night in 1944 was certainly one to remember for the residents of the 'Blue' as the John Bull Arch was struck for a second time in a matter of days, this time approaching eleven o'clock at night. Four were killed, with casualties just touching fifty. Blast damage was bad again and the confectionary factory, Shuttleworth's, was badly damaged.

Central Peckham was struck on 19 November, just behind the Post Office in the High Street. Nine people were killed as a V-2 hit the small residential Hardcastle Street. The post-war buildings in and around Peckham Hill Street and Marmont Road confirms this incident.

So, a lull in incidents prevailed as November turned into December 1944. As the residents of London were planning Christmas and hopefully looking forward to a brighter New Year, Hitler was planning something else – an offensive on the Ardennes in a desperate attempt to split the Allies, drive to the Channel and secure much-needed fuel supplies. But first, Southwark had several early Christmas presents to deal with.

With the Germans on the back foot in Europe, it was time for the Home Guard to stand down. Set up in 1940, these gentlemen, many First World War veterans, were prepared to put their lives on the line for the second time of asking should their homeland be invaded. In the last couple of years, their duties changed to such activities such as manning anti-aircraft batteries and searchlight batteries. Their new roles released younger service personnel who were required on the Continent. Also, bomber air raids were a thing of the past, the only threat coming from V-2s, which the Home Guard was powerless to deal with.

On 6 December, Varcoe Road, just south of South Bermondsey station, was hit. The incident was a Camberwell one technically, but there was blast damage in Bermondsey also. Eighteen people were killed in Varcoe Road and neighbouring Credon Road, including two-month-old David Booth, his three-year-old brother and his mother.

Sixteen people were killed at the junction of Lawson Street and Great Dover Street when a V-2 crashed into the housing there on the 14th. Well over 100 people were injured. Lawson Street has been literally wiped off the map as it no longer exists due to the modern housing estate that is in its place today.

On 16 December, Hitler kicked off his Ardennes offensive, more commonly known as the 'Battle of the Bulge'. There were early successes for Germany as thick fog prevented Allied air activities. As the weather slowly improved, the offensive withered despite fierce fighting. By the end of January, Hitler's last gamble was complete. With fuel a huge problem, many tank crews had to abandon their vehicles and walk back to Germany.

Before Christmas lunch could be eaten and 'Auld Lang Syne' could be sung to ring in 1945, the final V-2 visit of the year was delivered on the boundary of Southwark and Camberwell, on the junction of Albany Road and Bagshot Street, just a little way north of where Burgess Park stands today.

The V-2 struck around 7 p.m. on 17 December in this residential area. Special Constable Cecil Wallace and colleagues from Peckham police station were dispatched to the scene. On arrival, they split up to search the destroyed and damaged premises.

Wallace was told that there were people trapped in No. 128 Albany Road. Wallace went in, accompanied by a young man (who was never identified), and they quickly found one of the residents, George Seager, unconscious under a pile of debris. Mr Seager was carried out of the house in a short time.

The young man was convinced that there were further trapped people in No. 128, so Wallace went back in despite warnings from a local warden that debris was on the move and the building was becoming seriously dangerous. The young man was right as Wallace heard groaning coming from the area from where he had freed Mr Seager; it was an elderly woman, hanging by her feet from the damaged floor of the room above. As he was trying to move her, the floor above began to give way and she collapsed on top of him.

It was now impossible to go out the way he came in, so Wallace made a hole in a hanging ceiling and located the cellar door; therefore, he was able to carry the woman out to the waiting warden. The woman was Harriet Seager, wife of George, but despite Wallace's best efforts she died on 28 December of her injuries.

A further noise took Wallace back into No. 128, where he located a badly injured and trapped dog, which died as he was trying to free it.

Wallace was then told that there were further casualties in No. 126. He had to find his way into the premises via No. 124 and made a hole in the wall through which he was able to crawl. In the basement of No. 126 he found two teenage boys, who were only slightly injured, and he was able to bring them out to safety.

Quite a remarkable day's work for a Special Constable!

Fourteen people were killed in the incident with a further two, including Harriet Seager, dying in hospital of their injuries.

Many buildings were damaged beyond repair. The area today is part of the Aylesbury Estate and Burgess Park.

Camberwell decided to cut its Civil Defence for the New Year as it was no longer needed on its current scale. Incidents, although generally serious, were not an everyday occurrence. The compliment was reduced by about a half.

The end of a hard summer, autumn and midwinter arrived in the shape of Christmas 1944. Lives had again been changed due to the V-weapons. London would never look the same, and there was still more misery to follow, but with the Allies continually driving the Germans out of occupied Europe, there was a big light at what had been an extremely long and very dark tunnel.

The site of Courage Brewery's garage on the junction of Lafone Street and Tooley Street which was hit by a V-1 on 11 August 1944. (Southwark Local Studies Library)

The modern-day junction of Lafone Street and Tooley Street. (Author's collection)

Mayor of Bermondsey George Loveland, the second mayor of the borough to die in office in the war years – but his death was from natural causes. (Southwark Local Studies Library)

Drawing of the scenes after a V-1 hit McKerrell Road, Peckham, on 19 June 1944. (Southwark Local Studies Library)

The grave of Joan Clark in Camberwell Old Cemetery, killed by the V-1 strike on W. S. Thompson's factory on Peckham Rye on 22 June 1944. (Author's collection)

The grave of June Samouelle, killed by the V-1 strike on W. S. Thompson's factory on Peckham Rye on 22 June 1944. (Author's collection)

The modern shops are testimony to the V-1 that hit the Co-op in Lordship Lane on 5 August 1944. (Author's collection)

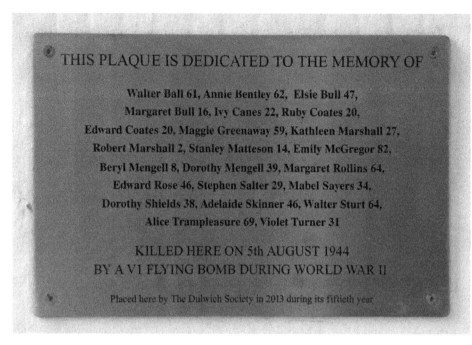

THIS PLAQUE IS DEDICATED TO THE MEMORY OF

Walter Ball 61, Annie Bentley 62, Elsie Bull 47,
Margaret Bull 16, Ivy Canes 22, Ruby Coates 20,
Edward Coates 20, Maggie Greenaway 59, Kathleen Marshall 27,
Robert Marshall 2, Stanley Matteson 14, Emily McGregor 82,
Beryl Mengell 8, Dorothy Mengell 39, Margaret Rollins 64,
Edward Rose 46, Stephen Salter 29, Mabel Sayers 34,
Dorothy Shields 38, Adelaide Skinner 46, Walter Sturt 64,
Alice Trampleasure 69, Violet Turner 31

KILLED HERE ON 5th AUGUST 1944
BY A V1 FLYING BOMB DURING WORLD WAR II

Placed here by The Dulwich Society in 2013 during its fiftieth year

Plaque to those killed at the Co-op in Lordship on 5 August 1944. (Author's collection)

The restored Lordship Lane Baptist Chapel, damaged by a V-1 in 1944 as described by Yvonne Wakefield. (Author's collection)

The site where the V-1 damaged Lordship Lane Baptist Chapel. The prefabricated house on the spot again is a reminder of the damage done during the Blitz. (Author's collection)

An old photo of the King's Arms public house in East Dulwich Road, finally destroyed by a V-1 in 1944. (Southwark Local Studies Library)

The clubhouse of the Dulwich & Sydenham Golf Club which was destroyed by a V-1 on 26 June 1944. (The Dulwich & Sydenham Golf Club)

1945
The End, but Still a Sting in the Tail

The capital endured its coldest spell for fifty years in January 1945, and with the cold, coal stocks ran low as many people, particularly the elderly, were forced to traipse some distance for a few scraps. Also, with the extreme cold the power companies were forced to reduce pressure by 10 per cent.

Building repairs were hampered by the cold spell, although Bermondsey and Southwark expected to be finished by April. Camberwell had a labour problem – a shortage of workers. Plus it was realised that more houses than thought would have to be pulled down rather than repaired.

Despite their precarious position on two fronts, the Germans were still in no mood to let London relax. On 4 January, a V-2 experienced an 'air burst', that is to say 'blew up over the skies of East Dulwich'. The falling fragments caused a little damage, but young ARP messenger, Reginald Wallace, died the following day from his wounds received in Lordship Lane.

At just after 5 p.m. on 6 January, a V-2 fell on Court Lane opposite Dovercourt Road in the leafy part of Dulwich, near the park.

Rescue workers found a young mother, Mrs Holland, with a baby in her arms and two injured children, Patricia and Judy Holland. Both were whisked away to the hospital. Sadly, Patricia died of her wounds.

James Holland had popped out to make a telephone call. As he heard the blast, he rushed back to discover that his house took the brunt of the strike. His wife was killed as the V-2 impacted.[i]

In total, seven people were killed, and there is evidence of repairs in the vicinity. The Dulwich Society has also had a plaque erected near the point of impact in memory of those killed.

Horsman Street was a small residential street that ran parallel to the railway between Urlwin Street and Bethwin Road. In the early hours of 14 January, nine people were killed as a V-2 blasted the street. Among the victims were four members of the Verrey family at No. 11.

Moser's factory stood on the junction of Marshalsea Road and Borough High Street. Moser's were a well-known local employer. As the workforce were clocking off after another day, at 5.15 p.m. on 22 January a V-2 thundered into the factory. The blast was huge; St George the Martyr was badly damaged, as were many of the shops in the immediate area. Thirty-five were killed in the strike, male and female employees; the youngest was Rosemary Rowland, aged fifteen. The workforce comprised employees from all parts of London as well as the local employees.

The following day, hundreds of miles away, the Red Army had reached Germany on the River Oder. Four days later, they liberated Auschwitz and uncovered the horrors within. The net was now closing.

Moving into February 1945, a big blast at mid-morning on the 14th on the junction of Waite Street and Trafalgar Avenue caused the deaths of eighteen. Twelve four-storey houses were demolished. Among the seventeen dead, there were two members of Women's Voluntary Service, living in the same block – Eleanor Dean, and Grace Easton along with her husband, Sidney, who had served in the Home Guard. A further seventy-eight people were injured.

With a general election due in the spring, election fever was brewing, with candidates jostling for position with post-election and post-war promises.

The last German forays into the three boroughs came in March, all in Bermondsey.

In the early hours of 3 March, Moodkee Street was hit by a throwback to the previous summer, a V-1. No deaths occurred. Later that day, at 11.10 p.m., the Dockhead Roman Catholic Church in Parkers Row took a direct hit from a V-2. Were killed immediately three members of the clergy: Fathers Finbar MacCarthy, Michael O'Riordan and Stephen Spillane. The nuns from the attached convent were fortunately not in residence at the time of the incident

The church had 'pancaked', just like the Jolly Gardeners in Union Street.

The rescue services were quickly on the scene, including Ted Hemming. Ted had been a part-time rescue service member in the early part of the war, while working as a milkman. When his milk depot was destroyed, Ted went full-time with the rescue service and attended many incidents.

There was an idea that someone was trapped under the wreckage. Ted was up for the task and set about finding a way into the wreckage. To reach Father Arbuthnot, Ted worked almost upside down for a gruelling three hours; the rescue was compounded by the injuries the Father had received and he was unable to help himself or Ted to remove a beam across his body.

Miraculously, the rescue was secured as Ted brought the Father out through the way he had burrowed in. Ted was exhausted, and he collapsed after his superhuman effort. Father Arbuthnot was rushed to the hospital, and a rumour went out that he had died, and Ted was mortified at this rumour. However, the rumours were false and he and Ted were firm friends for life.

This was the last major incident in the three boroughs. By early March the Allies had occupied Cologne and the Rhine was crossed at Remagen.

Bermondsey lost its second mayor within four years; Councillor George Loveland died suddenly on 11 March. He was devoted to his work, particularly Civil Defence, and had been chairman of the Emergency Committee. At the funeral, the Rector of Bermondsey, Revd Fisher, paid tribute, saying, 'He gave his life to Bermondsey. Bermondsey was in his blood, his heart, his mind.'

Loveland's widow, Florence, quite fittingly, was elected the new mayor.

John Smith, believed to be the country's youngest ever aldermen, was twenty-one when elected in Bermondsey. It was sadly reported that he was killed on 24 March while serving with the Glider Regiment, Army Air Corps. He is buried in Reichswald War Cemetery.

As preparations for a variety of victory celebrations were in the offing, one *South London Press* reader was erring on the side of caution. In a letter to the editor, the anonymous reader wrote,

Sir – I hear that very expensive restaurants are being booked for 'V Night'. Champagne is to flow freely and people intend to make a solemn evening a drunk and hysterical Saturnurbis. If this is so, then I call it shameful. I would suggest something more different to this, something more appropriate and more decent.

All churches should be open and we should all enter them and give thanks to God and pray for the safety of our men still fighting ... let us be English for goodness sake.[ii]

In April, with victory approaching almost by the hour, the government gave the country the 'thumbsup' for full street lighting to return. Air raids were now a distant memory, if not a forgotten memory for the families of the victims and those bombed out.

The Allied march across Germany continued apace as the German army on the Ruhr was encircled by the Americans. Hanover soon fell. The Russians, in the east, were sweeping all before them, taking Vienna and preparing for their assault on Berlin.

By the end of the month all resistance in northern Germany had collapsed, Dachau was liberated and Mussolini was executed by the Italian Resistance.

30 April was one of the biggest days in world history; Adolf Hitler took his own life in his bunker, along with Eva Braun.

On 8 May, Germany surrendered. Father O'Donahue of St Thomas More's Church, East Dulwich, was able to write in his church notice book several days later, 'Thanks to God that the war ended on May 8th.'

London was now set for a massive VE party on the 8th. Louise Sedgewick remembered, 'We had entertainment. They got a piano out. Most of the wartime songs; Rule Britannia, Tipperary, Run Rabbit Run. There were games for children and races.

Joe Scala deserted from his Air Sea Rescue base in Norfolk to get home for VE day. On his return, nobody even knew he had gone.

Ivy Malan rekindled the mood. 'It was tremendous! Oh, it was marvellous! Everybody was dancing, kissing one another, you know, arm in arm – it was really fantastic!'

As people awoke with sore heads the following morning, in the cold light of the day, thoughts were turning to the troops still fighting in the Far East and the horrors that had occurred in the concentration camps.

Enemy action had cost their lives of 2,700 civilians of the three boroughs; these are broken by borough as follows:

Bermondsey	701
Camberwell	1,014
Southwark	985

A further set of notable statistics was the decline in the population of the three boroughs from 1931 to 1951. There was no census in 1941.

	1931	1951
Bermondsey	111,542	60,640
Camberwell	251,294	179,777
Southwark	171,695	97,221

New towns, new prospects and new beginnings offered new hope.

VE Day party in Southwark Park Road. (Southwark Local Studies Library)

Cartoon of the Bermondsey Borough Council water cart used to water the Allied airfields in Holland in the run up to victory. (Southwark Local Studies Library)

The gargoyle from the House of Commons that somehow found its way onto the rebuilt Millpond Estate, Jamaica Road. (Author's collection)

VE Day celebrations in Nutfield Road, Peckham. (Southwark Local Studies Library)

VE Night in the Pyrotechnics' Arms, Nunhead. (Southwark Local Studies Library)

The candle-holders in St John's Church, Goose Green, which serve as a memorial to the six parishioners of the church killed in the war. (Author's collection)

Singer and 'Forces' Favourite' Anne Shelton lived in Court Lane, Dulwich. (Author's collection)

St George's Roman Catholic Cathedral in the final stages of its rebuild in 1958. (Southwark Local Studies Library)

The Blitz was responsible for exposing the remains of the Bishop of Winchester's Palace in Bankside. (Author's collection)

Appendix

The Rotherhithe Roll Chorus

For we like a lark down in Rotherhithe,
It's a cheery place to be.
For they are not too posh in Rotherhithe,
For the likes of you and me.
We all say,
Watcher, matey, ''oware getting on?'
Go on with you, get along with you.
So why not roll along to Rotherhithe?
And do the Rotherhithe Roll with me.

Reverend John Palmer's 'The Rotherhithe Roll' was first performed in 1939 at the youth club at Katherine's church, Eugenia Road. It was described as Rotherhithe's equivalent to the 'Lambeth Walk'. It consisted of a good deal of 'slapping' your partner and strutting around with thumbs stuck in the waistcoat.

Notes

1940: The Blitz Cometh

Daily Express, 9 September 1941
Letter to Southwark Local Studies Library
iii The Story of Reporting Post 12-AH Pullen
A Shout Into The Night-Thomas S Winter in Southwark Local Studies Library
Personal account in Southwark Local Studies Library
Pullen
vii *Sunday Pictorial*, 10 February 1952
viii Personal account in Southwark Local Studies Library
Bubbles of the Old Kent Road-Cyril Fluck
Southwark Local Studies Library, Oral History Project
South London Press, 14 March 1941
xii Letter to Southwark Local Studies Library
xiii St John's East Dulwich, Church and Parish-Mary Boast
xiv Boast
South London Press, 9 December 1940
xvi *Irish Independent*, 12 May 2009
xvii *South London Press*, 15 December 1940
xviii Letter to Southwark Local Studies Library
xix Westbury's Cane Works private papers

1941: A Deadly Spring

South London Press, 13 March 1941
South London Press, 21 March 1941
iii South London Press, 29 April 1941
South London Press, 2 May 1941

1942 and 1943: The Middle Years

South London Press, 13 February 1942
Various issues of the South London Press, March 1942
iii Various issues of the South London Press, June 1942
South London Press, 7 November 1942
South London Press, 29 January 1943
South London Press, 10 March 1943
vii South London Press, 10 June 1943
viii South London Press, 3 September 1943

1944: Small and Large Packages

South London Press, 21 January 1944
Letter to Southwark Local Studies Library
iii South London Press, 10 May 1944
The History of St James' Church, Bermondsey
Letter to Southwark Local Studies Library
Anonymous account, South London Press, 20 June 1944
vii Letter to Southwark Local Studies Library
viii Duden's Wharf-anonymous account
Reminiscences of Peckham and East Dulwich-Yvonne Wakefield

1945: The End, but Still a Sting in the Tail

South London Observer, 12 January 1945
South London Press, 4 April 1945